ORCHARDS

JONATHAN LATIMER

Orchards

Through the Eyes of an Artist

LANGFORD PRESS · 2005

Text © Jonathan Latimer, 2005
Foreword text © Dr Roger Key
Dr. Heather Robertson
Illustrations © Jonathan Latimer, 2005

Langford Press,10 New Road,Langtoft,
Peterborough,PE6 9LE
www.langford-press.co.uk
Email sales@langford-press.co.uk

Designed and typeset in Cycles by Nye Hughes,
Dalrymple, Edinburgh
Printed and bound in Singapore under the
supervision of MRM Graphics Ltd, Winslow

A CIP Record for this book is available from the
British Library

ISBN 1-904078-08-7

For Anna

Her Vitality
Beauty
Common Sense
And Deep Love

Contents

Acknowledgements

This book would not exist without the help of some very special people. For allowing access to their land, and providing welcome refreshments, good advice, practical assistance and some very useful information, I would like to thank orchard owners Fran and Brian Robbins, James Marsden, David Powell, Carol Westlake, Ian Wyatt, Liz and Neil Barker, Harry and Beryl Rushton, Mr and Mrs Williams, Tom Aspden, Colin Hinksman, John and Hilary Draper, Mr Morgan-Jones, Geoff Wilkinson, Will Whittal, Roger Wilkins, Stewart Wellings, Mrs Bentley-Taylor and Sue Welsby. In addition, I would like to make special mention of Liz and Tony Gentil, and for their kindness and warm hospitality, shown to me on many occasions.

The staff at Knight's Cider, the Hereford Cider Museum, Weston's Cider, Newton Court and the Somerset Rural Life Museum all gave freely of their time and provided practical help during my visits. Fieldwork was assisted by, or further information was gleaned from, Nigel Matthews of the Kent Wildlife Trust, Duncan Ashcroft of the Environment Times, Phil Rainford from the Northern Fruit Group, Joyce Morris of Creative Minds, George Henry Green, David Norman, Ced and June Davis, Avril Lynch, Catriona McLachlan, Barrie Juniper, Pam Seddon, Brett Westwood, Ian Mclean and Martyn Ainsworth, whilst Mike Johnson at Broome Farm helped enormously with fruit identification and specimen collection. Thanks to Kate Lloyd, Chris Fairs, and Moira and Fiona Pendry for looking at early drafts of text and making some very useful suggestions.

I would like to thank fellow artist John Cox and his wife Paula for their good humour, encouragement, advice, and a much-needed critical eye when progress was slow and difficult on occasions. The award of a Bursary from the Society of Wildlife Artists has made an invaluable contribution to my fieldwork and to the further development of my career, for which I am very grateful indeed.

A special thanks to Chris Fairs for his enthusiasm and practical help given in arranging access to countless Herefordshire orchards. The additional assistance that he has provided in supplying technical, historical and anecdotal information via phone calls and countless emails has been immense. Thanks to Ian Langford for his faith in my work, and the patience he has shown in watching this book develop since our initial meeting and embryonic discussions during the autumn of 2002.

Finally, to my family for their love and support, especially my Grandad Horridge, who did the most to encourage my drawing and appreciation of the natural world from an early age and who has probably had the most profound effect upon my subsequent career choice.

My final and biggest thanks to my wife Anna, for the love, patience, encouragement and support she has given me, without which this book could never have been published.

Foreword

Orchards give us nature on a human scale. They do not have the grandeur of our mountain scenery or the exhilaration of Britain's breezy coasts. Instead, orchards have a tranquil, domestic, beauty. Their essence is contained within the small precious things of our lives – fruit for our health and enjoyment, drink to warm us, shelter for our farm animals and bursts of blossom to please our senses. But orchards are also home to creatures of the ancient wildwood, though these inch-high 'stags' found in orchards, fit the scale of their surroundings. These beetles and their many relations see no difference between their prehistoric woodland habitat and our planted orchards. Birds of woodland and forest edge have followed the insect colonizers into orchards. Green woodpeckers probe for ants in the old turf between fruit trees, nuthatches and tree creepers bob about on tree trunks, searching for invertebrate prey within the bark.

Jonathan Latimer expertly guides our appreciation of the wonderful wild side of orchards as well as illustrating their human characters. His exquisitely detailed paintings, animated sketches and fascinating stories are illuminated by his passion for his subject and his art. The jewelled body of the noble chafer beetle, the flicker of a butterfly's wing and the fine ripeness of an apple are all beautifully captured in the following pages. *Orchards – Through the Eyes of an Artist* is indeed a book to treasure, as the orchards themselves deserve to be, now and in the future.

Dr. Heather Robertson
Lowland farm Ecologist, English Nature

Dr Roger Key
Senior Entomologist, English Nature

AUGUST 2005

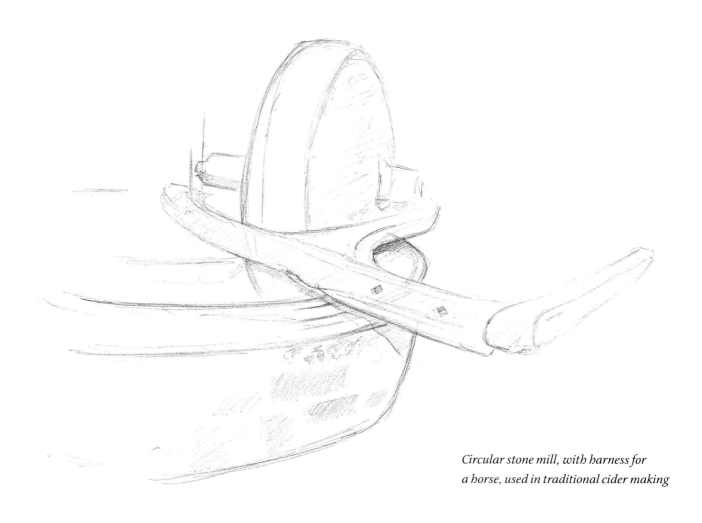

*Circular stone mill, with harness for
a horse, used in traditional cider making*

Introduction

In the simplest terms, an orchard can be defined as 'an enclosed garden of fruit trees'. Such a description, whilst remaining entirely factual, does little to convey the enchanting nature of these fascinating places. From commercial fruit plantations to neglected wildlife havens, and practically everything in between, orchards are endlessly inspiring. This book is a visual celebration: a journey of discovery through the eyes of an artist exploring the landscape, wildlife, people and produce that make orchards such a rich and interesting subject.

A pictorial study of orchards would obviously appear incomplete without illustrating the apple and its blossom, but many of the paintings included here reflect a more personal response to the life within an orchard. Some of my ideas have developed through discussions with the people I have met, and later described in this book, many of whose lives revolve around the orchards in their care. Other material is more documentary: simple sketchbook extracts or more detailed works inspired by the way the light played across a particular landscape. In its entirety, the artwork portrays a personal journal over a two-year period, illuminating a subject of which I had limited prior knowledge. During this time I have become more aware of the beauty of orchards, their complexity and importance in our changing natural landscape. With a richness that no single book could reflect, they are areas of special significance, places that deserve to be treasured and preserved for future generations.

As a point of interest, all the paintings were completed using Daler-Rowney Cryla acrylics. A variety of pre-stretched watercolour papers were also used, in addition to Daler-Rowney CS2 hot-pressed watercolour board.

Gazetteer

This list provides a chronological record of some of the places I have visited during the preparation of this book. Following many hours of research, my journey proper began with a trip to Dumfries and Galloway in late autumn. Since then, I have visited both public and private fruit collections, nature reserves, museums, and Apple Day events across the country, in a bid to portray orchard life in Britain in a detailed and visually exciting way.

2002

November 26 — Apple Orchard, Wigtown, Dumfries and Galloway

2003

February 5 — Weston's Cider Guided Tour, Much Marcle, Herefordshire

6 — Hereford Cider Museum and Weston's Cider

7 — Rural Life Museum, Glastonbury, Somerset

April 12 — Damson Day, Lowe Farm, Lyth Valley, Cumbria

14 — Whittingham Orchard, Lancashire

19 — Briarfields, Aston, Cheshire

May 6 — Briarfields, Aston, Cheshire

June 7 — Gregg's Pitt Orchard, Lyne Down Farm and Awnells Farm, Much Marcle, Herefordshire

8 — Awnells Farm and Woodredding Farm, Much Marcle Knight's Cider, Storridge, Worcestershire

July 11 — Nursery Farm, Eccleston, Lancashire

August 4 — Nursery Farm, Eccleston, and Hoghton Post Office, Lancashire

13 — Highgrove and Millennium Green, Eccleston.

14 — Bates Farm, Eccleston, and Horseman's Farm, Heskin, Lancashire

26 — Briarfields, Aston, Cheshire

September 9 — Bates Farm, Hilton House Farm and Nursery Farm, Eccleston, Lancashire

13 — Victorian Gardens, Orchard Conference, Tatton Park, Cheshire

16 — Hilton House Farm, Eccleston, Lancashire

24 — Doddington Apple Orchard, Cheshire

27 — Apple Day, Briarfields, Aston, Cheshire

October 15 — Woodbury Farm and The Standards Orchard, Moccas; Lower House, Preston on Wye; Alton Court, Dilwyn; and H.P. Bulmer, Lower House Farm, Staunton on Wye, Herefordshire

16 — G. Morgan Jones & Son, Sugwas; Risbury Mill and Risbury Court, Newton Court and Treasures, Leominster; The Hyde, Ivington; and Broome Farm, Peterstow, Herefordshire

17 — Standards Orchard, Moccas

18 — Hereford Museum Cider Festival, Woodredding Farm, Weston's Cider, Much Marcle, Herefordshire

19 — Brogdale National Fruit Collection, Kent, and Tewin Orchard, Hertfordshire

November 12 — Rural Life Museum, Glastonbury; Wilkins' Farmhouse Cider, Mudgley; and Rich's Farmhouse Cider, Watchfield, Somerset

December 6 & 7 — Bishop's Palace Orchard, Ripon, North Yorkshire

2004

January 1 — Bishop's Palace Orchard, Ripon, North Yorkshire

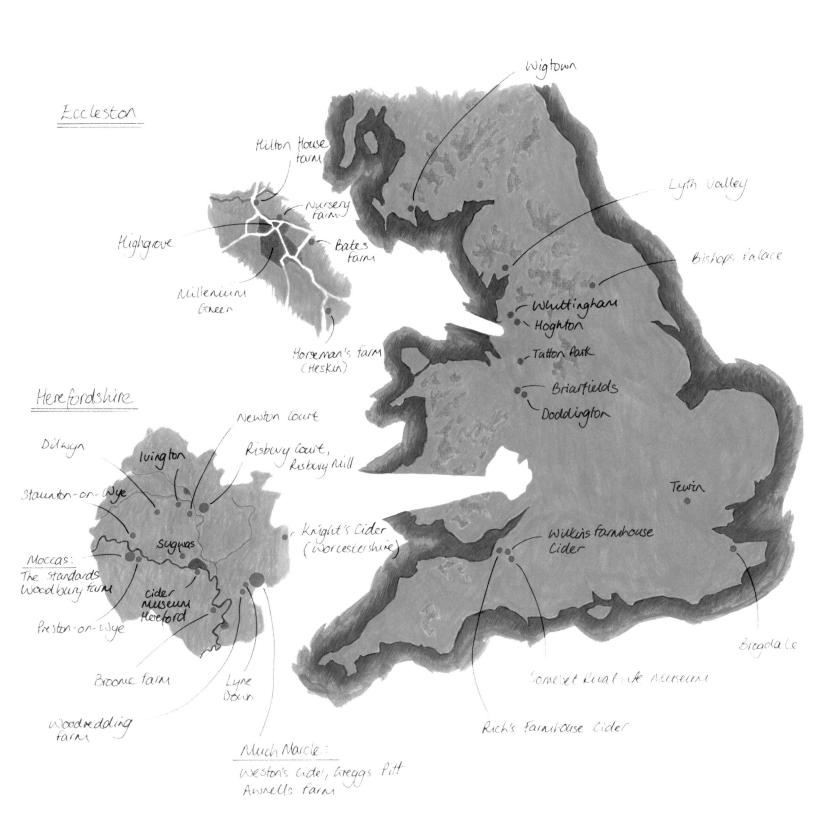

Eccleston

Wigtown

Hilton House
farm

Nursery
farm

Highgrove

Bates
farm

Millenium
Green

Lyth Valley

Bishops Palace

Whittingham
Hoghton

Horseman's farm
(Heskin)

Tatton Park

Briarfields
Doddington

Herefordshire

Newton Court

Dilwyn

Ivington

Risbury Court,
Risbury Mill

Staunton-on-Wye

Sugwas

Tewin

Knight's Cider
(Worcestershire)

Wilkins Farmhouse
Cider

Moccas:
The Standards
Woodbury farm

Cider
Museum
Hereford

Preston-on-Wye

Broome farm

Lyne
Down

Breapdale

Woodredding
farm

Somerset Rural Life Museum

Much Marcle:
Weston's Cider, Greggs Pitt
Awnells farm

Rich's Farmhouse Cider

The native apple (*Malus silvestris*) can still be found in suitable woodland habitat today. This small and bitter fruit was planted by Druids, in areas close to their sacred oak groves. The tree served as a host for mistletoe, an important plant in pagan ceremonies. Unsuitable for eating, these apples were regarded as sacred. The ancient Celts used them to produce a primitive fermented drink, the first British cider.

Cultivated apples were unknown in Britain before the Roman invasion in 55 BC. Roman army veterans were given settlements as an inducement to stay in a country seen as barbaric and with miserable weather. These would include somewhere to plant fruit trees – the traditional orchard was introduced to Britain. These orchards, a large paddock near the farmhouse, were ideal for keeping geese and chickens. Grazing beneath the trees, these birds reduced natural pests and enriched the soil. The Romans also introduced honeybees. Kept within the shelter of an orchard, they helped pollination and provided the additional benefits of honey and wax.

The first large-scale orchards producing fruit for sale were planted after the Norman Conquest. The Normans had a strong tradition of fruit cultivation and cider making, and introduced cider made with apples specifically grown for the purpose. These cider orchards would often be attached to abbeys and monasteries, with some of the fruit being sold to the public, whilst cider was produced from their own private presses. For the first time, monastic records listed different varieties of fruit. Costard and Pearmain apples were both recorded by the early thirteenth century. The Doomsday Book, in 1086, mentions old pear trees, planted by the Romans hundreds of years before. These were important features of the landscape and used as boundary markers.

Although fruit cultivation had spread widely under the Normans, the Black Death and the War of the Roses led to its serious decline. It was not until 1533 that Richard Harris, fruiterer to King Henry VIII, began a large expansion programme. He imported fruit from France and planted a model orchard at Teynham in

Kent. From here, trees were distributed to other growers. As fruit cultivation became more popular, its commercial value soared. This led to the planting of larger orchards in the southern counties, where warmer climates guaranteed effective ripening. Apples were planted extensively in Kent, and at its peak the 'Garden of England' produced around a quarter of Britain's eating apples, as well as vast quantities of cherries. In the West Country, many orchards were planted to satisfy the demand for cider making.

The demand for fruit grew following the industrial revolution, in line with population growth. As canals were built in the late 1700s, cider could be distributed further afield. Ten thousand hogsheads (1.1 million gallons) were exported annually from Worcestershire alone. By the 1850s the new railway system offered quick and affordable transport from orchard to markets in the city. The creation of new strains was encouraged by public demand, and by the end of the century, 2000 apple varieties were listed.

Food shortages during the war years greatly increased the profitability of home-grown fruit, producing ready-made markets for both small and medium-scale producers. The increase in the commercial value of such traditional orchards was generally short-lived. During this time, farmers were under pressure to produce sufficient quantities of food for a population effectively under siege from patrolling German U-boats. The war years perhaps led not only to the end of an era for traditional orchards but also to the most profound changes in land use this country has ever seen. Intensification and mechanisation on an unprecedented scale affected the British countryside for ever.

In many orchards the traditional standard trees were replaced by faster-maturing bush specimens, which are easier to manage and harvest. Planted in closely packed rows, such specimens can effectively treble the yield per acre. Bearing fruit in their third or fourth season, bush trees remain productive for about 30 years, compared with the longer-living standards, which produce a heavy crop after eight or nine years. Bush orchards are vastly more productive but far less rich in terms of biodiversity. With more intensive management and a shorter commercial life, they fail to provide the dead wood that is essential for insects, nesting birds and roosting bats. Pressure on land use from industrial and housing development, the lack of profitability of locally grown fruit and the increasing import of fruits have all affected orchard acreage. In the last 60 years some counties have lost almost 90% of their orchard coverage. Many areas have become little more than patches of green concrete, certainly in terms of conservation value.

Quite apart from their importance for wildlife, orchards hold a unique place in the nation's historical and cultural heritage, and some traditionally managed standard orchards do remain. These small areas, farmed in sympathy with the environment, continue to form havens for nationally important species of insects and birds. Many farmers have a genuine concern for, and interest in, wildlife welfare, and plant new orchards, making an important practical contribution to encouraging greater biodiversity. Organisations such as Common Ground are helping to promote an interest in the long-term preservation of these special places. With the dedication of sympathetic landowners, the sight of blossom-filled orchards in spring will hopefully remain an enduring sight in the British countryside.

Self-Sufficiency

Self-sufficiency

Since Norman times, animal husbandry has helped to maintain orchards. In mixed farming systems, grazing animals help to control the grass while fertilizing the soil. Cattle are turned into the orchard first, pulling up the long grass with their tongues. Sheep follow later, as they cope successfully with the resultant shorter turf. Grazing by geese is also encouraged, though the part they play in cropping the orchard sward is much less significant than that performed by larger livestock. Later in the year, as summer gives way to autumn, pigs feed noisily on the windfalls littering the orchard pasture. Damaged fruit, which would otherwise be left to decay, is enjoyed by the animals, and has the added benefit of enriching the flavour of the meat.

Free-range hens, like these Warrens belonging to Tony and Liz Gentil, provide fresh eggs on a daily basis. As they scratch beneath the trees, feeding on insects, worms, and the pupating grubs of pest species like the codling moth, these birds provide an organic form of pest control – an important ingredient in the orchard system.

alert expression

Honeybees

Honeybees are reluctant to fly in cold weather, and today, in early May, there is much more activity from the hives at Briarfields than on my previous visit just a couple of weeks ago. Tony and Liz Gentil have kept bees for the last 10 years, fulfilling an ambition held since before they were married.

Bees are the chief natural pollinators of fruit trees in Britain. For hundreds of years, hives have been placed in orchards during blossom time, since apples, pears, cherries and plums all require adequate pollination to ensure high yields of good-quality fruit. Today, the honeybee plays a vital role in fruit production across the globe, as beekeepers hire their hives to fruit growers during the spring. In addition to ensuring a successful fruit harvest, the bees also provide distinctive blossom-honey and beeswax.

The hives at Briarfields are situated in a small, grassy paddock, and remain there all year. During winter the bees gather in the lower parts of the hive, where they cluster around the queen to keep her warm. The bees collect nectar and pollen, which is utilised by the growing larvae. Stored nectar, mixed with enzymes in the bees' saliva, turns to honey, an alchemical process providing an energy-rich food source to keep the bees through the winter. During the late summer, many of the bees die, reducing the demand on this essential food store. In August and September, honey is removed from the hive, and is replaced with a substitute mixture of sugar and water to ensure that the bees survive the winter months.

In May, the pollen levels are quite low, and although there is no honey to be collected, it is fascinating to see the internal structure of the hive, as layers are removed one by one. The hives at Briarfields are both traditional WBCS, a style devised by beekeeper William Broughton Carr, at the turn of the twentieth century.

Honey

Man's association with these fascinating creatures is not limited to the benefits they bring to fruit growing. In the form of honey, bees produce one of the best natural sources of energy. This sweet, sticky fluid has a high easily digestible sugar content, which is readily absorbed. Claimed to have beneficial effects on both the heart and the nerves, honey is especially useful for the elderly and the infirm. Honey was so highly prized by the ancient Egyptians that sealed pots were often placed in burial chambers, to provide a source of food for the afterlife. Their faith in the longevity of the honey was justified – stores discovered within ancient tombs are completely edible after more than 2000 years.

Another valuable resource is beeswax. Formed as a by-product of honey production, it constitutes the scaffolding of the colony, and is used to cap honey stores within the hive for harder times ahead. On a commercial level, beeswax is important in the cosmetic and pharmaceutical industries, and is also used in artists' materials, furniture polish, and candles.

Tools of the Trade

Worn as part of a full suit, the gauntlet is a vital piece of beekeeping equipment and gives the hands complete protection against bee stings. Honeybees are not overtly aggressive creatures but are well documented for their altruism, and they will become agitated if the hive is disturbed.

The smoker is used to subdue the bees without harming them. This allows safe access and inspection of the hive. A container, traditionally made of copper, holds a slow-burning fuel such as cardboard or sack-cloth. Once lit, the user is able to regulate the amount of air available to the fuel with hand-operated bellows, in theory controlling the amount of smoke generated. In practice this type of smoker can be difficult to light, and the amount of smoke produced is hard to control. Often the smoke will cease completely at inappropriate moments, and beekeepers then have to stop what they are doing, which is less than ideal. This type of smoker is widely used today, although a more efficient design seems long overdue. The different designs available do make attractive collectors' items.

Silver Dorkings

The Dorking is one of the oldest of all domesticated breeds of poultry, dating back at least 2000 years. Originally brought to Britain by the Romans, the breed is widely appreciated as an excellent table bird. Dorkings are extremely attractive visually, the cockerel sporting a rich red comb, pied body and brilliant white shawl. Most birds have four toes: the first pointing backwards, and the second, third and fourth digits facing forward. The Dorking is unusual in having a fifth toe, which may possibly be used as a defensive spur.

This distinctive fowl can be found in the cider orchard beside the Rural Life Museum at Glastonbury, Somerset, which was planted by The Showerings Orchard Service, in the late 1970s and early 1980s. The company offered specialist grafting, pruning and disease prevention advice for local growers, and assisted the museum at the planning stage. A variety of cider apples were chosen to best represent a traditional farmhouse cider orchard. Thus, a range of sharps, sweets, bittersweets and bittersharps, which harvest early and late, were selected. The fruit is utilised in several practical ways, including traditional cider-making demonstrations each October at the museum.

Silver Dorking cockerel
Somerset rural life museum,
November 2003

Hereford Cattle

Hereford cattle are large but very docile animals. As their name suggests, this breed evolved from the indigenous red cattle that roamed the Welsh border marches. There are records of the breed being found in the county of Herefordshire for over 400 years. Throughout that time, they have played a part in the development of the county's orchards.

Hereford cattle produce beef of excellent quality, which, combined with a placid temperament, has ensured the breed's popularity with farmers at home and overseas. Exported to areas as diverse as Arctic Canada, and the arid lands of Australia, they continue to thrive in almost every corner of the globe.

Young Hereford calf. Sketched in early June, during one of several visits to Awnells Farm, in the village of Much Marcle, Herefordshire.

© Jonathan Latimer 2003

Awnells Farm

Awnells Farm is owned by David Powell, and has been in his family for over 70 years. Incorporating 220 acres of grassland, stocked with a large Hereford herd, the farm is of particular interest to me owing to its large orchard, in which the cattle are allowed to graze for much of the year. I visit the orchard for the first time with David's friend, and cider- and perry-producing neighbour, James Marsden. James works full time for English Nature, and I have travelled to Gregg's Pit, his own orchard deep in the Herefordshire countryside, to meet him. The opportunity to see cattle within a working Herefordshire orchard is an exciting prospect for me, and is something I have been keen to document, as a reflection of orchard life in the heart of this cider-making county.

The orchard trees are huge. This is a completely different landscape from the shorter, neatly cropped bush orchards I have seen previously. In this traditional standard orchard, the trees that dominate the landscape remind me very much of the mature parkland at Tatton Park, the National Trust property in Cheshire. Awnells farm boasts a mixture of cider apples and perry pears, with the orchard having the distinction of being registered by The Soil Association, the main body responsible for registering organic farms and food in the UK. David is a keen and active conservationist, and has close associations with the Countryside Restoration Trust. The charity, formed in 1993, is dedicated to the protection and restoration of the countryside, where high-quality food is produced using farming methods that encourage wildlife and enable people to earn a living from the land.

Despite the parkland appearance of this mature

orchard, it is possible, upon close inspection, to discern that the trees are planted in a regimented pattern, a typical feature of all standard orchards. There are gaps, where aged or dying trees have finally succumbed to a fierce winter storm. Others, still standing in part and having been reduced to little more than metre-high stumps, provide convenient scratching posts for the cattle. The majority of the trees that remain may be over 100 years old, and as we walk through the orchard, James is keen to point out the telltale signs of several other orchard inhabitants. Woodpecker-chiselled holes adorn many of the trees, whilst numerous decaying trunks provide roosting sites for bats and a residence for a host of small invertebrates. A rich array of birdlife, including woodpeckers, tree sparrows and starlings, make use of these arboreal, statue-like relics for nesting,

with bountiful feeding opportunities provided by the complex ecosystems that their decaying boughs sustain. There are buzzards here too, whilst in early spring, wild daffodils and primroses flourish on the orchard floor. With careful consideration and management, such biodiversity is not difficult to achieve.

Harvest Time

Although cattle and other livestock are free to roam the orchard and graze for most of the year, during harvest time they are removed to feed on adjacent pasture. This has the purpose of protecting the crop, as well as preventing the animals overindulging on the autumn bonanza of fruit. Stock will usually be removed at least four weeks prior to harvest, but eight to ten weeks before the fruit is picked is probably more realistic. In cider and perry orchards, especially those of the smaller producers, fruit is left to drop naturally to the ground, where it is later collected by hand. With heavy branches drooping within the animals' reach, cattle would readily consume as much fruit as they could. Once apple picking is complete, livestock can be turned back into the orchards, providing there is sufficient 'keep'. These young calves were sketched in mid-October, on pastureland at Sugwas in Herefordshire, a farm belonging to Morgan Jones & Son, whose orchard produce is supplied to Hereford-based H.P. Bulmer, now part of the Scottish Newcastle group.

Young Hereford Calf.
October 2003

Female & 1st male ♂
pied wagtails feeding on cattle manure

Woodredding Farm

Nestled on a hill, giving panoramic views across the fields towards Much Marcle, lies Woodredding Farm, where Brian Robbins and his wife, Fran, have lived for the past 10 years. The farm comprises a standard cider orchard, which covers an area of about two hectares, with the hundred or so trees producing a crop of between 10 and 15 tonnes of fruit each autumn. The orchard here is entirely organic, and is registered as such by The Soil Association. In addition to having the orchard inspected each year, Brian also submits an annual report to demonstrate that non-approved sprays or fertilizers are not used on the land. Although the farm deeds show that an orchard was present on the site some 200 years ago, most of the existing trees have been planted in the last 70 years, with the crop being sent to local cider makers, Weston's, in Much Marcle.

Gloucester Old Spots

Gloucester Old Spots have been known as 'orchard pigs' for many years, as they were often kept in the cider orchards of the West Country, grazing in summer and gorging on windfall apples in the autumn. Legend has it that such behaviour led to the pigs acquiring their distinctive black spots, which were originally bruises resulting from the impact of falling fruit. Although the breed has only enjoyed full recognition since 1913, it is likely that the pigs have existed since at least the early 1800s. After suffering a marked decline by the 1970s, Old Spots are now classified as endangered by The Rare Breeds Survival Trust, and have fared much better recently, thanks largely to the enthusiasm of a few dedicated farmers.

Like all pigs, Old Spots feed in a noisy, rather hurried manner. In a bid to seek out every morsel, the Old Spots loosen the turf with their robust snouts. Such behaviour not only improves aeration of the soil, but also accelerates the decay of leaf litter. In addition, it helps with pest control, disturbing the larvae of nuisance insects like codling moths and cockchafer beetles. Disturbed patches of earth are examined under the watchful eye of Brian's free-range hens, which are ready to pounce should any potential meal be overlooked.

As I watch the pigs, I am reminded of a similar partnership between bird and beast that is still played out today within the remaining fragments of ancient forest in isolated parts of Europe. The wild boar, formerly widespread in Europe but hunted to extinction in Britain by the seventeenth century, is similarly an efficient and effective digger, foraging for beechmast, acorns and roots within the litter. Disturbed pockets of humus present an inviting opportunity for woodland birds, like finches and tits, to feed on previously hidden invertebrates.

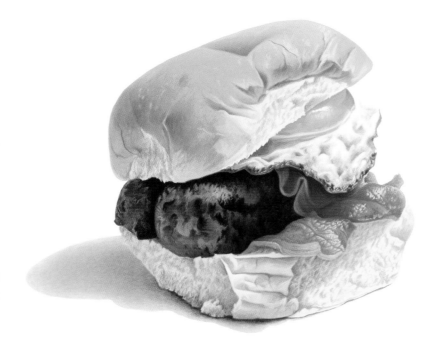

Having fed the animals, Brian and I spend some time chatting about his work, and I ask him about the pigs and their long-term chances of survival. 'Trying to convince people that eating rare breed meat is the best way of conserving the animals is quite a difficult argument for some town dwellers to accept. Most rural folk know a bit more about the economy, and appreciate that this is the case.' With a growing movement for eating free-range produce from animals that have been fed and treated well, there is a ready market for Old Spot meat, and most of that from Brian's animals goes to Newent butcher, Paul Gurney.

Over coffee, I chat to Brian and Fran about their long-term plans for the farm. Adjacent to the farmhouse lies an old granary, housing a Victorian cider mill that would have been used to produce home-brewed cider. The building is being converted into two holiday cottages, whilst the mill, in a good state of repair, is to be retained as a feature when the work is complete. While undertaking my research, I have been impressed by the help and hospitality afforded me by farmers and homeowners alike. Humbling at times, the afternoon spent at Woodredding Farm has been no exception.

Brian and Fran also run The Scrumpy Pig, a mobile catering unit selling home-produced sausages and bacon at local shows and food fairs, including the annual Food and Drink Festival, held each September in Ludlow, Shropshire.

Portland Sheep

Early November in Somerset, and the cider harvest is in full swing. The cider orchard at the Rural Life Museum, Glastonbury, presents a completely different picture now. During the depths of winter the trees were stark and bare, devoid of foliage. Only a smothering of golden-yellow lichen adorned their naked branches. In autumn, the trees look incandescent in the early morning light, their leaves a brazen collection of golden browns and reds. The orchard floor is carpeted with fallen apples, greens and russets of every shade, dew-covered and marble-like. In winter, only the nameplates on the trees gave an indication of their variety, and so, today, it is immensely satisfying to see the unfamiliar fruits, like Tremletts Bitter and Yarlington Mill. The 21 trees in the orchard include 18 distinctive varieties.

As in traditional orchards, farm animals keep a check on the grass – though the orchard is not large enough for cattle. In addition to a goose and a couple of Aylesbury ducks, several Silver Dorkings scratch under the trees. Two sheep graze in contentment – these are Portlands: a rare breed, named after the island in Dorset where the Saxons traded wool. They are impressive animals, and I spend some time sketching them in the warm, late autumn sunshine.

Fruit for the Table

Fruit for the Table

The British have had a love affair with fruit growing since the Romans first crossed the Channel over 2000 years ago. Damsons and cherries, apples and plums, cobnuts, pears and quinces all find their place within the fruitful British landscape. Away from the cider- and perry-producing counties of Britain, the main commercial areas for fruit production include Kent and Worcestershire, with Cumbria, Cheshire, the Home Counties and East Anglia all playing an important role in providing fruit for the country's palate and culinary imaginations.

In spite of economic and political pressures reducing the profitability of many commercial operations, interest in fruit growing, at least on a small scale, is increasing. The desire to buy locally grown produce, advocating the benefits of traceability and distinctiveness, is helping to revive the traditions of the past. As the days become warmer and the blossom fills the trees, anticipation of another year's rich bounty grows. If the trees are spared a late spring frost, the lengthening days of summer provide cherries, plums, pears and apples in infinite variety. Eaten straight from the tree, or transformed into homemade pastries, pies, jellies and jams, the harvest can be savoured into the depths of winter. The incredible diversity of locally grown fruit provides inspiration for many, and is a gift that deserves to be valued and cherished by all.

The Lyth Valley

At Lowe Farm in the Lyth Valley, the annual Damson Day celebrations take place in early April, an event organised by the Westmorland Damson Association. Closely related to plums, damsons are more tolerant of the colder, wetter weather than many other varieties of fruit, and have been grown successfully on the heavy, clay-rich soils in this corner of Cumbria for at least 300 years.

Between the limestone scarps of Whitbarrow and Scout Scar to the west of Kendal, the Lyth Valley is a glorious place at blossom time. The undulating agricultural landscape, with its sheep-filled fields and clustered farmsteads, surrounded by meandering stone walls and hedgerows comprising blackthorn and damson trees, makes this part of Cumbria distinctive. In early April, when the majority of deciduous species still retain their naked winter forms, the damson trees display their profusion of dazzling white blossom, brightening up the local landscape.

Damson trees seem to border every road, stretching along intersecting hedgerows and between scattered farm buildings as far as the eye can see. The air is crisp and clear, filled with the early morning melody of a dawn chorus. The resident song thrushes, collared doves, robins, wrens and chaffinches are joined by the plaintive call of a single willow warbler, newly arrived from sub-Saharan Africa. From across the lane and low-lying pastureland beyond comes the bubbling song of a curlew, whilst the raucous calls of a pair of carrion crows alert my attention to a passing buzzard high above. The solitude and tranquillity of the early morning is a magical experience.

Although the majority of damson trees in the Lyth

Valley grow individually or in small isolated pockets of land, there are the more traditional, formal orchards here too. Leaving the main road to join a narrow lane that winds its way along a wooded ridge, I find a small 'plantation' of 20–30 trees in the corner of a secluded field. Beneath the canopy, a single blackbird and a couple of redwings are feeding busily. Predominantly winter visitors, redwings are similar in size to starlings, and are the smallest member of the thrush family to commonly occur in Britain. Although about 50–100 pairs breed in the highlands of Scotland, most of the UK population arrives from the breeding grounds in Scandi-navia during October and November. By the end of March, these attractive birds will largely have left Britain for the upland birch forests of northern Europe, although occasionally birds linger into April and even May. Without any obvious sign of predators in the vicinity, the birds are flighty and appear nervous, frequently leaving the orchard floor for the safety of the canopy above. Although redwings, and their larger cousins, fieldfares, are frequently encountered within cider orchards, as they gorge on piles of windfall apples, the juxtaposition of these individuals with the blossom-filled boughs of spring is an exciting and unexpected visual delight.

Damsons

Damsons originated in the Middle East around Damascus, in present-day Syria. Exactly who introduced them to our shores remains uncertain, though damson stones have been found in excavations around the sites of Roman camps. The fruits were certainly part of Roman life, with their skins being used for the manufacture of highly desirable purple dyes.

The Westmorland damson is named after the county that forms part of present-day Cumbria. It is thought to be a type of Shropshire prune. Although damsons are grown in other parts of the British Isles, including Cheshire and Shropshire, where they are a common feature of the countryside, the flavour of the smaller Westmorland damson is said to be second to none. The fruits are sold by the roadside and in local shops in September, and are used in a variety of products, from jams and jellies to wine and damson gin.

During the spring, sheep are turned into the orchards
to control the grass. Feeding alongside the animals are
several species of bird, including robins, thrushes and a
single pied wagtail, whilst a noisy group of starlings
inspect the close-cropped earth around a pair of resting
lambs for small invertebrates.

Damson orchard in early spring

Damson Day

Damson Day has become an integral part of the rural Cumbrian calender, organised by local people wishing to preserve the rich history and remaining damson orchards in this part of the country. Prior to the Second World War, carts sold fruit in the town of Kendal on Damson Saturday each October, with local railway and canal networks playing a vital additional role in the market, transporting cartloads of fruit to the jamming factories in Lancashire to the south. A staggering 250 tons of fruit was sold in Westmorland in 1938, when the first Damson Growers' Association was formed and established a small canning and village jam factory. A shortage of sugar and manpower in the Second World War caused its sad and rapid demise.

The gathered crowds eagerly anticipate organised walks through the blossom-filled orchards, but perhaps the main focus of the day's event is a small but bustling farmers' market. With a number of stalls taking up temporary residence within the farm courtyard, adorned with bunting and banners, there is everything on sale from damson cakes and jams, to pâté, pies and damson gin. There is a real buzz about the place, a tangible excitement in the air, epitomising the pride of the local community, which has worked hard to fight back after the devastating effects of foot and mouth, which ravaged the Cumbrian economy in 2002. With an increasing desire to purchase high-quality, locally produced and readily traceable food and drink, the opportunity to restore the fortunes of these famous fruits remains promising.

The warm and friendly atmosphere reflects the commitment of local people to reviving local traditions, and it is through the successful marketing of events like this that the Westmorland Damson Association hopes to return the damson orchards to their former glory. By increasing the profile of the Westmorland damsons, it is hoped that the interests of damson growers in the district can be safeguarded for very many years to come.

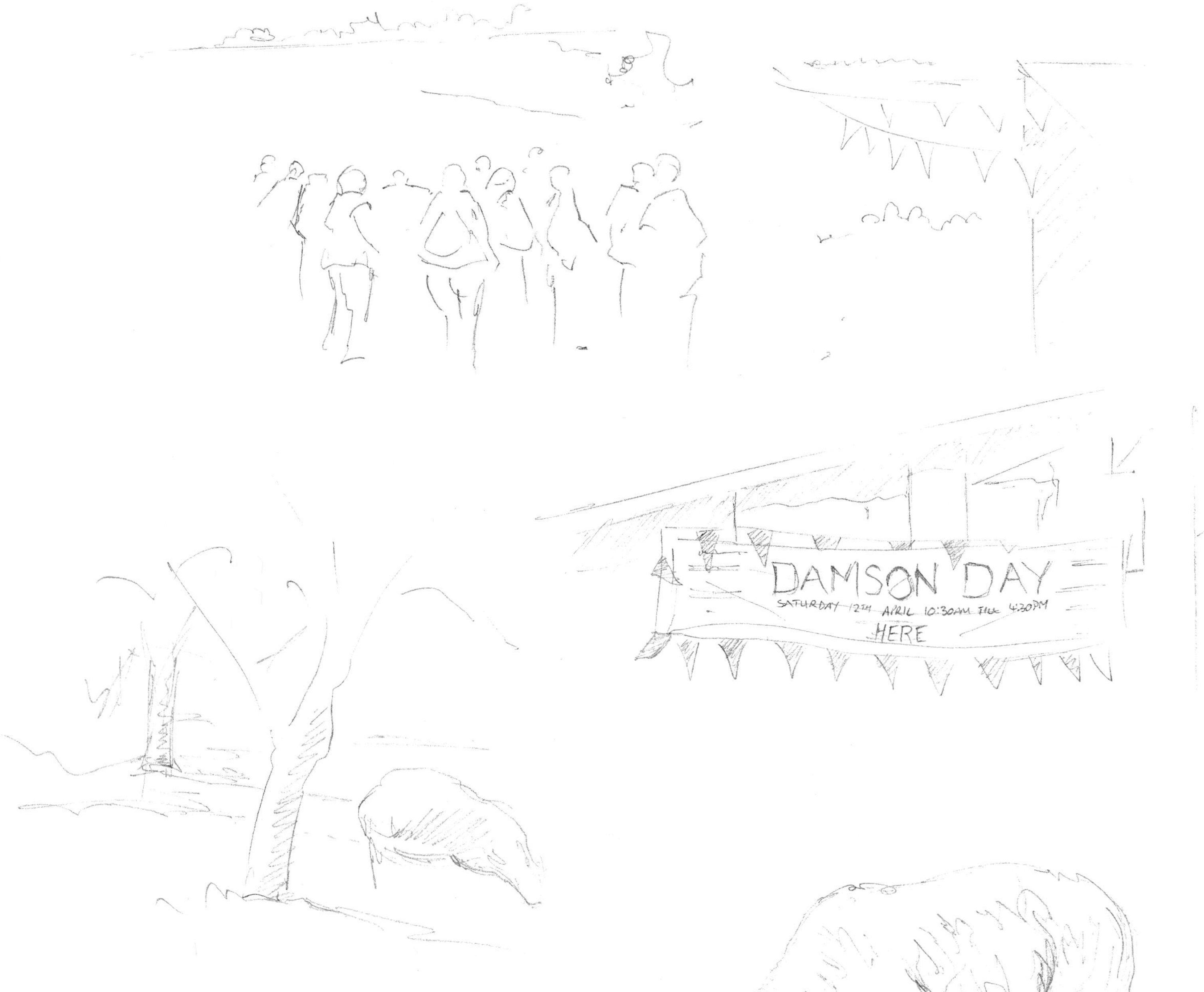
DAMSON DAY
SATURDAY 12TH APRIL 10:30AM TILL 4:30PM
HERE

Damson orchard in blossom

Whittingham Apple Orchard

The remaining apple orchard at Whittingham hospital, near Preston in Lancashire, is situated on land formerly comprising 34 acres of cultivated gardens on the 458-acre hospital estate. During their heyday in the 1950s, the gardens provided an almost daily supply of green vegetables, in addition to vast quantities of soft fruit, apples and pears. Documentation of food cultivation during the 12 months up to August 1959 includes nearly 6000 lbs of apples and 2120 lbs of pears, in addition to a staggering 137,162 lbs of cabbage, 48,558 lbs of carrots and 49,185 lbs of beetroot. Much of this vegetable production has long since ceased, although the orchard, which had suffered from years of neglect, has recently been tidied and pruned by hospital residents, under the helpful eye of Phil Rainford, from the Northern Fruit Group.

Orchard Losses

Before the introduction of cotton mills, the village of Eccleston, in Lancashire, was predominantly a fruit growing area. Parish maps of 1893 show over 40 orchards between this and the neighbouring village of Heskin. Until the 1950s the fruit was sold to traders from Wigan Market, about eight miles to the south. The former orchard at Whalley House Farm, above, disappeared 25 years ago, having come to the end of is natural life. With little incentive to replant, this six-acre site was grubbed to make way for permanent pasture. The annual harvest of pears was welcomed during the war years, when locally grown produce still had a reasonable commercial value, but since then many orchards have been neglected, or the land sold for housing development.

At nearby Hilton House Farm, Harry Rushton owns what is left of a similar-sized plantation. About 60 trees are all that remain of the original 200 Victorian plantings. There is a selection of apple and pear varieties, and a few damsons. Most of the fruit is left for his herd of Charolais cattle to enjoy, though damsons are still picked by Harry's wife, Beryl, for use in her homemade pies and jams. The trees that are still producing provide welcome windfalls for feeding butterflies, including several spectacular red admirals, which float lazily between the trees in the warm September sunshine.

The diagram opposite highlights the loss of commercial orchards in the UK, over a period of 27 years up to 1997. In 1970 there were 62,200 hectares remaining; by 1980 this had reduced to 48,700, and by 1997 only 22,400 hectares were left, a massive 64% overall decline. This trend continues, resulting in the disappearance of traditional varieties of fruit and methods of farming, which may be lost for ever. In particular, the decline of old orchards, which provide habitats for a wealth of wildlife, also threatens the UK status of many rare species, including beetles, mammals and birds.

* Statistics courtesy of DEFRA

Bates Farm

Against the usual trend, the orchard at Bates Farm, on the outskirts of Eccleston, has actually extended in size from the original plot featured on the map of 1893. This is due to the work of Tom Aspden, whose family have farmed the land for the last 43 years. By planting a variety of apples and pears in 1990, including Conference and Comice varieties, Tom effectively doubled the area of trees to about a third of an acre.

Enthusiasm for traditional fruit growing still remains, and this area, known as the 'Evesham of the North', is enjoying something of a renaissance. Thanks to the Eccleston Apple Blossoms project, many of the remaining orchards and trees have recently been documented and mapped with the help of Phil Rainford. The project compared orchard coverage in 2002 with an original map of 1893, visiting many of the remaining sites in addition to collecting memories from past and present owners. With funding provided by The Countryside Agency, Nationwide and the Heritage Lottery Fund, a booklet documenting the group's findings was published in 2004.

Although many of the orchard fragments that remain have become little more than romantic symbols of a bygone era, the project has been successful in raising awareness of the freshness and variety of locally grown produce. In a bid to celebrate this local distinctiveness, a community orchard has recently been planted in the Millennium Green, a public park at the centre of the village. With over 30 trees individually sponsored by local residents, it provides a lasting legacy of fruit growing in the area.

Highgrove Pears

Liz and Neil Barker live at Highgrove, in the village. In the late nineteenth century, the garden boasted an orchard of nearly 70 trees, many of which have long since died. Today 18 trees remain, mostly varieties of pear, including Hazel, Red Robbins, and a small, hard variety nicknamed 'Stones'. The Conference pears are still producing a good crop – Neil's father formerly sold fruit from these trees to the canteen at Leyland Motors.

In mid-August the garden is alive with the hum of bees and an assortment of other flying insects. Butterflies feed busily on the remaining rotting plums, which provide an important source of sugar at this time of the year. The trees have suffered from late spring frosts, and the summer crop has been poor. Several of the trees are coming to the end of their natural lives, producing little or no fruit. In time, their gnarled forms will be removed to make way for larger beds, or more of the soft fruit that has produced a bumper crop.

First recorded in 1827, the Hazel or Hessle Pear is a very hardy variety, thought to have originated from the village of Hessle near Hull in East Yorkshire. It is grown widely across the north of England and Scotland today.

Hessle Pear, (left)
Red Robbins Pear, (opposite page)

Cherries

Cherries were first introduced to Britain by the Romans, but were well known to the Greeks from at least 300BC. Although the Normans were responsible for propagating the fruits, following the invasion of 1066, it wasn't until the sixteenth century that serious cherry growing took hold in Kent, under the supervision of Richard Harris.

Today, Kent remains famous for its cherry growing. The large-scale, sheep-grazed orchards, which remain a distinctive part of the landscape, are under particular threat from development in the overpopulated South-East. These standard orchards, in which sweet cherries have traditionally been cultivated, attract large flocks of starlings and other birds during early summer when the fruit becomes ripe. Scaring devices, such as 'cannons', are frequently employed by growers, in a bid to lesson the destructive impact of these birds.

Owing to their huge stature, growing in excess of 40ft, these standard sweet-cherry trees, often of the Stella variety, require specialist pruning and can be difficult to maintain, in contrast to the more compact-growing acid or sour varieties. The most popular variety of sour or culinary cherry, the Morello, is grown on a commercial scale in the UK. Owing to their astringency, these cherries are generally used in processing, forming a constituent part of many jams, and in the manufacture of specialist wines. Until quite recently, the smaller culinary varieties were the only cherries that could practically be grown in an average-sized garden. The introduction of the Colt dwarfing rootstock, which enables trees to be restricted to a height of about 10ft, has allowed both sweet and sour varieties to be grown in a pot on the garden patio.

British Plums

With mild wet summers, Britain has the ideal climate for growing plums. The fruits that are familiar today are likely to be hybrids between the native common sloe and the cherry plum, which came from Central Asia and was taken to northern Europe by the Romans. Before Roman times, when there were around 300 varieties, the Greeks had taken cultivated varieties back from Syria, the traditional home of the closely related damson.

Around 12,500 tonnes of plums are grown annually in the UK, mainly in the South-East and around the Vale of Evesham in the West Midlands. For the last few years, the town of Pershore in Worcestershire has hosted an annual Plum Festival on August Bank Holiday. Like Damson Day in Cumbria, the festival began in order to boost interest in locally produced fruit and orchards, with a similar range of stalls and exhibitions packed with information and different foods.

Many different types of plum are grown in Britain today, though several varieties are rare and highly localised. The main commercial varieties are Opal, Victoria and Marjorie's Seedling, which are picked by hand. These varieties ripen in different months, from mid-July through to October, providing a steady supply. Whether classed as cooking or dessert types, these fruits are full of goodness, with high levels of Vitamins A and C, calcium, potassium, iron and fibre. They also contain phyto-oestrogens, cancer-fighting agents known to reduce the risk of heart disease and other serious health problems.

Marjorie's Seedling plums have purple skins and sweet yellow flesh, and make excellent jam. The white powdery film or bloom that occasionally covers the fruit is produced naturally as it ripens, indicating the freshness of the fruit.

Three British varieties (From the top) Victoria, Oullin's Golden Gage and Marjorie's Seedling Plums.

Bishop's Palace Orchard

An old standard orchard, on the outskirts of Ripon in North Yorkshire, sits within four acres of land that originally comprised the Bishop's Palace Estate, which was built in 1847. Despite being acquired by Barnardo's back in 1950, the orchard was largely neglected until the early nineties, when the Walled Garden Scheme was initiated. As part of Ripon Community Link, the scheme has given opportunities to young people and adults to take part in rewarding project work in the area. Help and direction from the Northern Fruit Group has enabled the orchard to be cleared of weeds and other debris, and it is now largely restored to its former glory. With a remaining 60 or so trees, the orchard encompasses an interesting mix of apples and pears, in addition to a number of Victoria plums, the most popular and commonly grown variety in the UK.

Beyond the orchard walls lies the former Victorian kitchen garden, itself having undergone a recent transformation. Vegetable production and other country skills have been taught on site. Alongside providing opportunities to learn woodland management and gaining certificates in carpentry, exciting plans for the future include building a teashop and craft rooms, together with expansion of the vegetable production through the erection of additional greenhouse space.

various stages of
ripening, all found on the
same branch.

Victoria Plums, Lancs.
August 2003

© J Latham

British Apples

From the Scottish lowlands to the south coast of England, some of the finest apples in the world are grown on British soils, and have been for nearly 2000 years.

Despite the fact that over 150,000 tonnes of apples are harvested each autumn, two-thirds of those sold in British supermarkets are imported. The meagre choice for the customer is very limited when measured against the 6000 apple varieties that have been cultivated in Britain over the centuries. Many remain no more than distant memories, from a time when flavour and local diversity was more important than perfect shape, even size and blemish-free skin. The demand for cosmetic uniformity has driven many orchards out of existence. When vast quantities of fruit not conforming to supermarket standards are left to rot, orchards represent an unprofitable use of land.

Scabs and blemishes may look unsightly, but the fruit remains fine for eating. Crisp and tasty, apples make the perfect healthy snack, providing an excellent source of vitamins and fibre, in addition to being free of sodium, cholesterol and fat.

Locally grown varieties are available at farmers' markets from early September, when the harvest begins in earnest.

From top: Ashton Bitter, Lord Derby (small), Galloway Pippin, Lady Sudeley

Brodgale National Fruit Collection

Apples are widely grown far from Hereford and the South-West, the areas traditionally associated with fruit cultivation. One of the most popular dessert apples today, James Grieve, was first recorded in 1893 and raised in Edinburgh by Mr James Grieve [facing page]. It received the Award of Merit from the Royal Horticultural Society in 1897, and a First Class Certificate in 1906. Available in September and October, it is a hardy and adaptable fruit, with a refreshingly sweet flavour and crisp, juicy flesh.

The Laxton Brothers of Bedford propagated Laxton Superb [right], another dessert variety, in England in 1897. In 1919, this apple received an Award of Merit, and in 1921, a coveted First Class Certificate. Grown on a commercial scale today, the variety was first introduced in 1922. Laxtons have a firm, sweet, juicy flesh, and are cropped in November.

These are just two of the thousands of varieties of apples and other fruits growing at Brogdale, home of the National Fruit Collection. In the 150 acres of orchards near Faversham in Kent, there are over 2300 varieties of apple, 550 of pear, 350 of plum, 220 of cherry, and 320 varieties of bush fruits, as well as smaller collections of nuts and vines. Guided tours round the fruit collections take place regularly throughout the day. During the Apple Day celebrations in late October, many fruits are available to taste and buy. Special events are organised throughout the weekend, including a display featuring a fascinating time line, featuring groups of apples exhibited in chronological order of their propagation.

British Pears

Pears have been cultivated for thousands of years, the Roman writer Pliny recording at least 39 distinctive varieties. The Romans may well have introduced the fruit to Britain, with the pears grown in this country being derivatives of *Pyrus communis*, a native of western Asia. Pear trees are longer lived than apples, and are less susceptible to disease and attack from pests. Prospering more readily in warmer climates, they are, however, prone to damage from spring frosts, which can destroy the early blossom, and so are frequently grown within the shelter of a protecting wall. Pears were widely cultivated in monastic gardens, with some of the best pears in the country to be found in the old walled gardens of country houses, like Ripley Castle, near Harrogate in North Yorkshire.

Dessert pears are widely used in cooking and stewing, and have a pronounced, sugar-rich flavour. For many people this taste is considered superior to even the sweetest apples. Their butter-like consistency, a unique texture alluded to in the names of many French varieties such as Buerre d'Amanlis, makes them a perfect culinary choice. The Conference pear, which produces a reliable, and heavy, late-autumn crop, is the most famous commercially grown dessert variety in Britain. Raised by Rivers of Sawbridge, this variety was named after being exhibited for the first time at the National British Pear Conference in 1885.

Another familiar pear is the Warden, one of the oldest varieties in cultivation and named after the Cistercian Abbey in Bedfordshire, where it was used in pies during the fourteenth century. Mentioned by Shakespeare in his play *The Winter's Tale*, the pear has rich historical ties with England, though the Romans may well have initially introduced it to Britain. Commonly referred to as the Black Worcester pear today, the 'warden' has appeared on the City's coat of arms since the reign of Queen Elizabeth I, when she saw the fruit growing at Whystone Farm in 1575. Its association with the county predates even this event, with references to it usage as a crest by Worcestershire bowmen in the Battle of Agincourt some 160 years earlier.

Doddington Apple Orchard

Doddington in Cheshire lies about four miles to the south-east of Briarfields, and boasts an apple orchard at the childhood home of Ian Myatt. Now living in Widnes with his wife Edna, Ian still owns and maintains the orchard on land his father Arnold bought back in 1921, from Sir Delves Louis Broughton-Bart of nearby Doddington Hall. Following the acquisition, four acres were planted with apple trees over a period of about 10 years, adding to a number of established pear trees and a single large apple situated to the rear of the property.

In its heyday, the orchard boasted about 1000 trees, both bush and standard, of at least 14 different varieties.

Living away from home and unable to devote sufficient time to the orchard, Ian reduced the acreage of trees following his father's death in 1972, by clearing the land and renting it to the local Bridgemere Nurseries for growing Christmas trees. The most profitable trees near the house were kept. Newton Wonder, Allington Pippin, Charles Ross and Bramley constitute the bulk of the apple crop. In late August, it is the peak of the apple harvest for the mid-season varieties that dominate. Ian is on site and, during this busy time of year, uses a static caravan as a base within the orchard grounds. The home in which he grew up remains, and is now leased to long-term tenants.

The Bramley is Britain's most popular cooking apple. It is sill produced from the stock taken from the original tree in Southwell, Nottinghamshire, which was planted by Mary Braidsford in the early nineteenth century.

eating apples collected the
traditional way by hand, using a
ladder propped up against the
tree.

Allington Pippins

J Lartime 03

Apple collecting at Doddington Apple
Orchard, Cheshire
September 2003

Leaving Ian to the rather labour-intensive task of fruit picking, I explore the orchard at leisure in the warm autumn sunshine. Butterflies are abundant here, represented by several species including the ubiquitous red admiral, comma and the odd small tortoiseshell, in addition to a late peacock, which I am surprised to find still on the wing. Feeding on the damaged windfalls lying in the dappled shade, the butterflies are at times difficult to spot.

With a yield of over 5700 lbs of fruit produced in the two previous autumns, the trees are doing well. This is due in part to the help Ian enlisted from ADAS, the National Agricultural Advisory Service. They made a thorough examination of the trees at Doddington, and collected soil samples for detailed analysis. The resultant action plan presented to Ian suggested that the addition of hydrated lime would be beneficial to the trees, to counteract the acidity of the soil. Applied in January, and followed with fertilizer in April, the resultant treatment has improved both the quantity and the quality of the crop.

Fruit sales begin in the last weekend in August, and continue well into December. Ian currently devotes two days a week to the orchard, and also attends the farmers' market in Nantwich at the end of September. Signs at the orchard gate attract passing trade, and the excellent fruit from this corner of Cheshire travels widely each autumn, with regular customers arriving from North Yorkshire and Nottinghamshire.

Red Admirals
— Tiverton, Devon
September 2002

Fiesta apples are of great commercial interest, owing to their consistently good cropping habit and excellent storage properties. This brightly coloured variety has a refreshing sweet flavour, and is usually ready to pick from mid-September.

Late Summer Apples

The fruiting season for apples begins in July, with varieties like Early Victoria ripening towards the end of the month. Other types, like Blenheim Orange, are not ready to pick until October. The storage period for apples is related to their picking time – the earliest ripening fruit requiring eating within seven days. Apples harvested in the late autumn will, if stored correctly, remain useable well into the following spring.

Late August in the paddock orchard at Briarfields, and the heady fragrance of fruit permeates the air. The first apples are ripe and ready to eat. There are 81 trees here altogether, and, as well as apples, there are pears, plums, apricots, quinces and walnut. The orchard was planted by Tony about 11 years ago and provides a home for a pair of geese and several free-range hens.

It is a dull, muggy day, and butterflies are very much in evidence, fluttering amongst the leaf litter. There are red admirals, speckled woods, a comma and at least a couple of painted ladies. This latter species is common in Britain, and is one of the world's most widely distributed butterflies. This tiny creature, with a wingspan of barely two and a half inches, migrates to mainland Europe from North Africa in the spring, reaching as far as Iceland to breed in the short northern summer. This feat of migration is awe inspiring, a testimony to the miracle of Creation.

At the furthest end of the paddock, between the hen house and the hedge, the ground is littered with fallen fruit. In the half-eaten remains of a Charles Ross, no doubt the work of one of the hens, a speckled wood feeds under the scrutiny of the ever-aggressive wasps. Unlike the many flies that are also present, the wasps seem to actively provoke the butterfly into giving up its feeding space, by agitating its wings. I am no expert in insect behaviour, but such aggravation seems to constitute some form of territorial 'brinkmanship'.

Apple Day

The enthusiasm of growers for the fruit they produce
and the orchards they care for is infectious. There is
often sadness, too, that so many varieties have been lost
through simple neglect, or to the insatiable appetite of
the plough. Cultural traditions, once passed with
reverence from one generation to the next, have also
been lost, a victim to the 'progress' made during the
latter half of the twentieth century.

Initiated by Common Ground on 21 October 1990,
Apple Day provides an opportunity to demonstrate the
richness of local food. The festivals encourage people to
take a greater interest in the origins of their food, with
the apple central as a symbol of physical, cultural and
genetic diversity. Apple Day events enable people to see,
taste and buy varieties of fruit that are no longer available in the shops, varieties that are, for some, little more
than distant childhood memories. Apple identification,
growing advice and pruning demonstrations encourage
a resurgence of interest in fruit propagation. From apple
chutney to homemade cider, there is much to eat and
drink, something for everyone to fire the culinary
imagination.

An astonishing success since its inauguration in the
early 1990s, Apple Day gains in popularity, promoting a
recognition of the contribution orchards make to
enhancing quality of life through the preservation of
local diversity and by providing rich wildlife refuges.
Apple Day shows that, with a little encouragement and
effort, we can all make changes for the better.

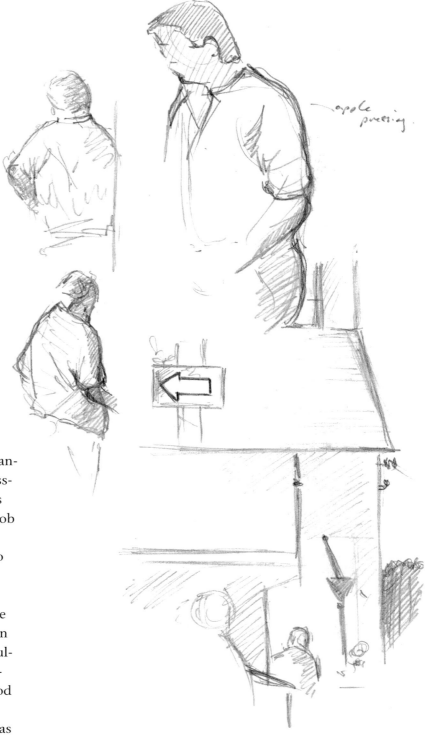

Briarfields Apple Day

In late September, Apple Day at Briarfields in Cheshire reflects the role of the orchard in community life. Tony and Liz Gentil have organised a variety of activities, including juice pressing, apple tasting, beekeeping demonstrations and willow weaving. Children are invited to bob for apples, a game once used to predict which child would be the first to marry. According to tradition, the quickest to get hold of an apple would be next to walk down the aisle.

There is also a garden party organised by the local village church, and ample refreshments in the form of a barbeque. Tony, a trained horticulturist, is on hand to assist with fruit identification, and, on this glorious sunny day, it is a good opportunity to explore the orchards, a private collection of over 400 varieties of apple trees, as well as pears, plums, quince, medlar, walnut, mulberry, vines, figs and other soft fruit.

At this time of year the variety of ripening apples is perhaps the biggest draw, including the impressive Norfolk Beefing [illustrated], a first-rate, old English apple, first described in the 1840s and used primarily for cooking and drying.

Wildlife

Orchard Biodiversity

Orchards can be rich wildlife havens, offering a patch-work of habitats that are attractive to many species of insects, birds, animals and plants. Traditional planta-tions, formerly an integral element in mixed farming systems, include woodland, meadow, hedgerow and pasture. Each habitat holds a unique collection of species, and when considered as a whole, they form areas of rich biodiversity.

The factor that makes mature orchards particularly attractive to wildlife is the presence of dead and rotting wood. With the exception of pear, orchard trees decay relatively quickly, allowing colonisation by cavity-nesting species such as little owls and great spotted woodpeckers. Secondary tenants like starlings and tree sparrows, two species whose populations have under-gone a recent, rapid decline, exploit disused wood-pecker nests in time. The importance of retaining such trees is clear, since both these birds are listed on the British Trust for Ornithology's (BTO) 'Red List', com-posed of species of high conservation concern.

Old fruit trees also provide valuable roosting sites for bats. Orchards with unimproved grassland and meadow, boasting healthy populations of insects like the cockchafer, may support several species, including the noctule and long-eared. Both are uncommon, although even the pipistrelle, Europe's most abundant bat, is in decline. Feeding areas being degraded through indiscriminate pesticide use is much to blame, although the destruction of suitable nesting sites, as 'unprofit-able' trees are grubbed and entire plantations disappear completely, compounds the problem.

Rot holes expose the internal heartwood to the elements, and along with fungal invaders comes an assortment of other wildlife – beetles, hornets, and wood-boring grubs. Bracket fungi grow slowly on the bark, which is also colonised by mistletoe, the parasitic plant revered by the Celts. Mistletoe berries remain a favourite of the mistle thrush, whilst the leaves of fruit trees are under constant attack from a myriad of insects, including the caterpillars of the stunning eyed hawkmoth.

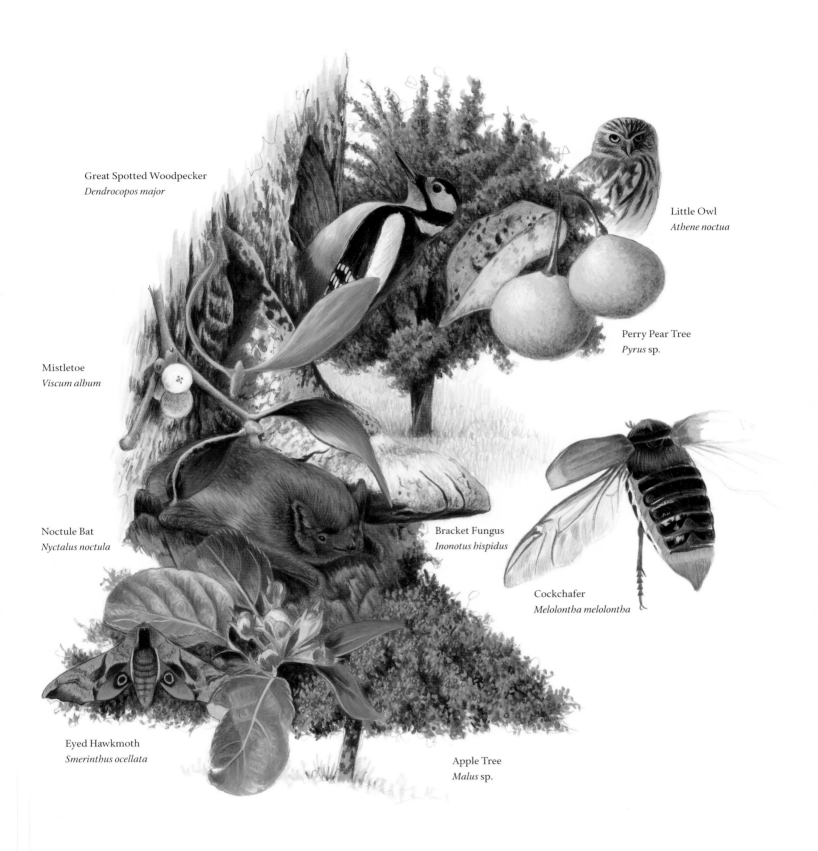

Great Spotted Woodpecker
Dendrocopos major

Little Owl
Athene noctua

Perry Pear Tree
Pyrus sp.

Mistletoe
Viscum album

Noctule Bat
Nyctalus noctula

Bracket Fungus
Inonotus hispidus

Cockchafer
Melolontha melolontha

Eyed Hawkmoth
Smerinthus ocellata

Apple Tree
Malus sp.

Orchard Meadows

Hay meadows and pastures were formerly an integral part of the farming system. They were specifically managed to support livestock, traditionally cut for hay in July/August and grazed during the autumn. With increased mechanisation, the need for hay diminished, since tractors replaced the work of horses, and many mixed farms converted to cereal production. The pressure to increase yields was perhaps greatest during the Second World War. Every bit of marginal land was turned over to agriculture, and, consequently, wetlands were drained and most meadows were ploughed up.

Over the last 60 years, farming has changed beyond all recognition. Government policy has encouraged farmers to constantly increase their outputs. Sheep and cattle are kept in higher concentrations to gain maximum profit from the land, and so most grassland is managed intensively to produce the best possible crop for direct grazing, or for the production of silage. Grass yields have risen 15-fold, to as much as 15 tonnes per acre, thanks to specially developed grass strains, in conjunction with the extensive use of artificial fertilizers and herbicides. Such 'improvements' have had a profound effect on local wildlife, producing grasslands of limited conservation value. Flower-rich pastures have become a rare sight in many parts of Britain, surviving only where intensification remains unprofitable due to poor fertility or inhospitable terrain.

Fortunately, through agricultural subsidy schemes, flower-rich meadows are being restored or recreated, replacing acres of monotonous green silage with vibrant, flower-filled fields. In the most profitable meadows, there may be as many as 45 species per square metre, including meadow foxtail, lady's bedstraw and the nationally rare snake's head fritillary. Even hay meadows with few plants species can provide food for seed-eating birds. Dandelion and sorrel are particularly valuable for redpoll, goldfinch and linnet. In addition, meadows, crucially left uncut until late July, provide a safe nesting habitat for ground-nesting species such as lapwings, curlews, yellow wagtails and skylarks. (Silage is cut too early and too frequently in modern grasslands to produce seed, or to allow birds to successfully rear their young.)

Unimproved, unsprayed, species-rich meadows are not only of interest in their own right, but act as reservoirs for biodiversity. Healthy invertebrate populations are important for birds, and under favourable conditions, populations are able to colonise new areas, including orchards. Species that would typically be absent from mature orchards expolit the rich feeding grounds and nesting sites that they provide, and may include yellow wagtails, barn owls and brown hares.

Meadow Butterflies

Hay meadows are essentially man-made habitats, by-products of traditional, low-intensity farming. They nevertheless form valuable habitats for many species of wild flowers, including knapweed, ragged robin, red clover and lady's smock. This latter species is a particular favourite of the orange tip, a striking butterfly that can be seen on the wing from March to July, but the occasional adult appears in late August.

Opposite: Areas of rough pasture, with an abundance of thistles, attract many butterflies, including the Painted Lady, and Peacock.

Hedgerows

Although many traditional orchards have disappeared, fragments of 'wild' plantations remain, remnants of orchards that may have occupied the same piece of land for many hundreds of years. Ancient hedgerows, perhaps initially planted as field boundaries, protect the trees from wind and frost, and comprise important natives such as alder, hazel, spindle and yew. Such hedges provide nest sites for yellowhammers, long-tailed tits, and summer visitors like the whitethroat.

In spring, dog rose, bramble, and blackthorn blossom attracts feeding butterflies, moths, hoverflies and bees. Later in the year, badgers, foxes, mice and voles gorge on the autumn bonanza of blackberries, haws, elderberries and sloes, in anticipation of leaner times ahead. Migrants like the whitethroat must lay down adequate fat reserves for the start of their long, southward migration, and so, prior to departure, they modify their feeding strategies to take advantage of the seasonal abundance of these energy-rich foods.

Bramble - blackberry, August 2004
(Rubus fruticosus)

Speckled Wood.
(Pararge aegeria)

Blackthorn (sloe), October 2003
(Prunus spinosa)

Apple Blossom

The first blossom on the trees is a welcome sight, a sure sign that spring has arrived. This floral bounty is a lavish advertisement to many insects, the petals signifying the prospect of a valuable source of energy-rich nectar. A variety of moths, wasps, butterflies, and hoverflies visit fruit blossom, and, along with the familiar honeybee, *Apis mellifera*, play an important role in pollination, especially in commercial orchards. Orchards with areas of adjacent rough pasture have an advantage, as these grasslands provide a home for many species of native bumblebees, which are perhaps the most effective pollinators of all. These large, generally social bees nest underground, frequently making use of disused mouse holes. Visiting up to 1000 flowers per hour and readily foraging during cold spring weather, these most active of natural pollinators are extremely welcome from the grower's point of view. There are 25 species in Britain, although some are uncommon and very localised.

Maintaining valuable nesting and feeding sites for these and other creatures is vital for the overall health of the countryside and areas associated with more commercial activities. Sustainable development calls for a greater appreciation of the importance of these individual habitats, and the wider role they play in maintaining the health of our complex, natural ecosystems.

Bullfinches

In addition to insects, fruit blossom, particularly the buds of pear, plum and apple, attract the bullfinch. This brightly coloured species was highly prized as a cage bird by the Victorians, and huge numbers were trapped. Many orchard owners welcomed its subsequent decline, but legal protection enabled the population to revive. Despite this, numbers in Britain crashed by about 41% between 1984 and 1991. The main reason for this seems to be a loss of suitable nesting habitat, particularly thickets and hedges. Herbicide use has compounded the problem, reducing the amount of suitable feeding sites. Bullfinches are now protected under the Wildlife and Countryside Act 1981. Under new licensing arrangements, which came into force in October 1996, trapping under general licence is permitted, but only in Kent.

Although the male is particularly brightly coloured, this dumpy, self-effacing finch is easily overlooked as it feeds unobtrusively in the canopy. Bullfinches have a low-pitched, discreet call, a rather melancholy 'phu', which is often the first indication that a bird is in the area.

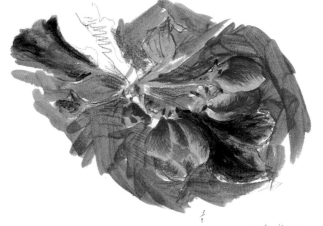

apple blossom — Ripon N Yorkshire
4 May 2003

bull necked
appearance.

looking away.

Male bullfinch. Ripon
December 2003.

Shooter

dumpy looking.

Wryneck

The wryneck is a strange bird, named after its ability to twist its head almost 180° without moving its body. Cryptically coloured relatives of woodpeckers, they have a high-pitched call reminiscent of a falcon, and plumage very similar to the ground-nesting nightjar. Having a preference for old woods and orchards, with associated old pastures providing a reliable source of ants, the birds' main food, wrynecks were formally widespread summer visitors to England. Although there is a historical trend of population decline in the UK, the birds' demise since the 1950s has been rapid, from a population of between 200 and 400 pairs to becoming virtually extinct as a breeding bird by the turn of the century.

Many former orchard haunts, particularly in Kent, have disappeared in the intervening period. Favourable breeding habitats do still exist in many areas, so the reason for the birds' decline appears mixed. With many orchards appearing to be perfectly suitable for supporting a reasonable-sized population, increased pesticide use, coupled with changes to habitats in some areas, may be the main cause of the birds' disappearance. Wrynecks are summer visitors to southern and central Europe, breeding as far north as northern Finland, and are birds that I have seen in both Hungary and Poland. Although Britain is at the extreme north-western edge of its current European range, birds can turn up almost anywhere on passage, and are most likely to be encountered on the east coast in late August and September.

Noble Chafer

The noble chafer symbolises much that is important about orchard conservation. In Britain, the adult beetle is dependent on ancient fruit trees, where its larvae develop in the rotting wood over a period of two to three years. The grubbing of old plantations, along with a reduction of nectar and pollen sources through inappropriate management of orchard grasslands, has led to a loss of suitable habitat, contributing to the species' considerable decline within its range. Despite being widely distributed in Europe, from Spain in the west to Hungary in the east and as far north as southern Scandinavia, the noble chafer has been rare in Britain for over a century.

Found in both apple and cherry orchards, the beetle appears to have a particular liking for plum trees. The remaining old plum orchards near Evesham and those in the Wyre Forest in Worcestershire constitute a remaining stronghold in the country. The adult beetles are very beautiful creatures, with iridescent wing cases, varying in colour from metallic emerald to deep bronze-green.

Bird sketched at
close quarters from
car at edge
of road ——

looking away

bird perched on
rubble mound
some distance
away

distinctive
pot bellied shape
when feeding

Red-legged Partridge.
7 June 2003.
Merle Ridge
Herefordshire

Marcle Ridge

Above the village of Much Marcle, Marcle Ridge provides a perfect place to enjoy the panoramic views across the Herefordshire countryside. To the north lies Ledbury, and the Precambrian Malvern Hills beyond. Some nine miles distant, to the south-east and skirting the Gloucestershire border, is May Hill. It is said that perry pears, from which the traditional fermented drink of perry is made, will only thrive within site of this distinctive local landmark. From my vantage point, arable land stretches as far as the eye can see in every direction, interspersed with wooded copses, meandering hedgerows and orchards of infinitely varying size. In an adjacent field, a red-legged partridge, a mixed flock of corvids, and three hares are feeding in the early evening light. It is good to see the hares here.

Although brown hares remain widespread and locally abundant in lowland Britain, numbers have declined by around 80% over the last 50 years or so, to a current population of around 1.1 million. With intensive farming and large cereal monocultures often dominating the agricultural landscape, the reduction of suitable feeding habitats has a dramatic negative impact on many species of animals and birds. Old, neglected traditional orchards become welcome havens for hares and other mammals, including foxes, badgers and deer.

Nuthatch

The nuthatch is a handsome and charismatic bird. With an almost fearless disposition, it is commonly seen climbing up or down the branches of deciduous trees with equal gusto, in an insatiable search for insects, seeds or nuts. They are common birds of mature orchards, deciduous woodland and large gardens, and this bird is depicted in a typical posture, pausing on the knarled trunk of a mature perry pear. Nuthatches nest in holes in trees, frequently plastering mud around the entrance until the desired size is reached. In time such cavities provide welcome nesting sites for secondary tenants, including blue tits and tree sparrows.

The latter species has suffered a serious decline in Britain over the last 25 years – as much as 95%*, probably due to an increased use of herbicides and pesticides. With a current breeding population in the region of 110,000 pairs, the tree sparrow is now listed on the RSPB Red List of *Birds of Conservation Concern*.

It is sometimes easy to dismiss the importance of old orchards as they come to the end of their 'profitable' life. The decline of tree sparrows, and the benefits that old orchards provide in terms of suitable nesting and foraging sites, should serve as a warning, highlighting the fragility of our ecosystems. Every time that mature trees are felled, or a traditional hay meadow makes way for agricultural monocultures, we denude the natural landscape of diversity and wildlife-rich communities. We do little more than substitute variety for uniformity, often leaving barren wildlife deserts in return.

* The Common Bird Census (CBC) indicates a decline of 95% in numbers in Britain between 1970 and 1998.

Nuthatch 20/10/03

Selection of lichen. Somerset Rural Life Museum apple orchard.

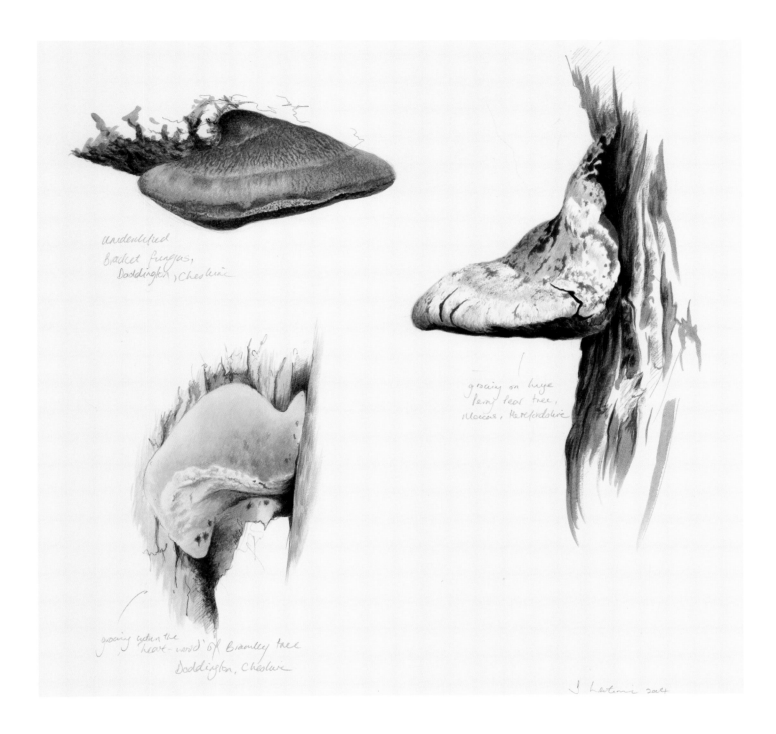

unidentified
Bracket fungus,
Doddington, Cheshire

growing on huge
berry pear tree,
Moccas, Herefordshire

growing within the
'heart-wood' of Bramley tree
Doddington, Cheshire

J Leslie 2004

Bracket Fungi

Many species of bracket fungi are tough and leathery, despite having a sponge-like appearance. The visible bracket constitutes the fruiting body of the organism, the mycelium living within the host tree. Unlike toadstools, most bracket fungi have pores rather than gills beneath their caps.

Fungi are the only organisms capable of digesting lignin, the organic substance of which wood is composed. As a result, they play a vital role in the decompo-sition of dead wood, and can commonly be found on the decaying remains of mature fruit trees, with certain varieties also encountered on living speci-mens. Some species support their own unique invertebrate fauna, including specialist beetles and fungus gnat larvae, and so the presence of these spectacular fungi on fruit trees can greatly increase orchard biodiversity.

These bracket fungi, despite varying greatly in appearance, are possibly specimens of a single species, *Inonotus hispidus*. This is probably the most usual bracket to be found in orchards.

Barn Owls and Bulmer's Cider

Barn Owls are usually associated with open country and farmland, their smaller cousin, the little owl, being more at home in the wooded confines and ancient hedgerows of old orchards. However, these five-week-old chicks were hatched in a specially made owl box on Bulmer's 400-acre cider apple orchard at Penrhos Farm, Llantilio Crossenny, Gwent.

Bulmer's, a corporate member of the Farming and Wildlife Advisory Group (FWAG), supports the local Herefordshire meetings. When the company purchases a new farm, FWAG carries out an environmental audit in a bid to maximise the biodiversity of the land. An annual review and action plan is drawn up by a local FWAG team for each farm under Bulmer's ownership. This includes hedge planting and maintenance, preserving ponds and wetland areas, and leaving field margins uncut. Such wildlife corridors are a natural hunting ground for predatory beetles and other invertebrates. These creatures perform an important natural pest control service, feeding voraciously on many species, including several moths that can cause serious damage to tree foliage and fruit.

Improving existing nesting sites for a range of wildlife is also an important aspect of the work. There are several hundred bird boxes within the company orchards, increasing the number of suitable nest sites for a variety species, including tree sparrows and starlings. Specialised boxes for bats and bumblebees are also erected, and, over time, new species are encouraged to use them, increasing local biodiversity with very limited effort. Commercial bush orchards often lack the rich diversity of wildlife that mature standard orchards contain. Although the dead wood and the rich wildflower meadows that are so good for wildlife may be absent, these orchards do not have to be the green wilderness that many modern farms have become. With dedication, forethought, and consideration, there is immense scope for increasing local biodiversity.

For all the help that FWAG may offer, little can be done to enhance or protect our rich natural heritage without the participation and cooperation of farmers and growers. Government legislation is needed to encourage the beneficial partnerships between wildlife and people on both a local and a national level – areas rich in wildlife are also rich for people. What price tag has a patch of ancient woodland, or how do you value the thrill of watching a barn owl hunt at dawn? The manner of our response to these questions will impact upon our environment for ever.

Little Owl
Mardle Ridge
Herefordshire - June 2003

Old orchards are a favourite habitat for
Little Owls, a species introduced to the UK
in the 19th century

Male Pheasant

elongated neck gives,
bird a strange,
almost
cartoon-like
appearance.

always 'intense' looking,
almost startled
expression.

fence post running across entire width of
orchard, between older 'standard' trees
and newer plantation.

Standards Orchard.
Marcle
Herefordshire.

October 2003

The Yaffle

Green woodpeckers are widespread breeding birds in Britain, favouring mature woods and parkland with open spaces in which to feed. Old orchards provide ideal haunts for this gawky-looking species, having areas of unimproved grassland habitat that support large populations of ants, on which the birds feed. Despite their large size and colourful plumage, green woodpeckers are frequently overlooked, as they spend much of the time feeding unobtrusively on the ground. They are shy and wary birds; the first indication of their presence is often an explosive rendition of their shrill, yaffle-like call, from which the bird derives its country name.

During a fortnight in October 2003, I saw more green woodpeckers in old orchards than I had seen in total over my previous 18 years of birdwatching in the UK. Whilst such an observation remains completely unscientific, it surely demonstrates the importance of orchards for these wonderful birds.

Greater Stag Beetle

The greater stag beetle, *Lucanus cervus,* is the UK's
largest terrestrial beetle, reaching seven centimetres in
length. With its giant, antler-like mandibles, the male is
arguably the most spectacular-looking invertebrate in
Britain. This species requires habitats with an abundant
supply of decaying wood or fallen logs. It is within such
rotting timber that the larvae develop over a period of
four years, before pupating and emerging as adults at
the beginning of the flight season the following year.
Although the species remains widespread in parts of
southern England, the fact that the beetle grubs take so
long to develop means that they are extremely vulner-
able to the clearance of dead timber. Since mature apple
trees, *Malus* spp, are one of the most likely trees to
harbour this uncommon insect, the preservation of old
orchards remains a priority.
 The clearance of dead wood is likely to be one of the
chief factors why this species is in decline, and as a
result it is listed as a priority species under the UK
Biodiversity Action Plan (UK BAP). This is the UK's
initiative to maintain and enhance biodiversity, with
English Nature and other organisations from across all
sectors being committed to achieving the Plan's
conservation goals over the next 20 years and beyond.
Across its range, including central and southern Europe
eastwards to Japan, the species is included in the Red
Data lists of a number of countries where it remains
rare or is in decline. The international trade in insects
presents a particular threat to unusual and spectacular-
looking species like *Lucanus cervus,* and, as a result, the
beetle is protected under Schedule 5, Section 9.5 of the
Wildlife and Countryside Act 1981. This legislation
prohibits all trade in the species, violation of which can
result in prosecution.

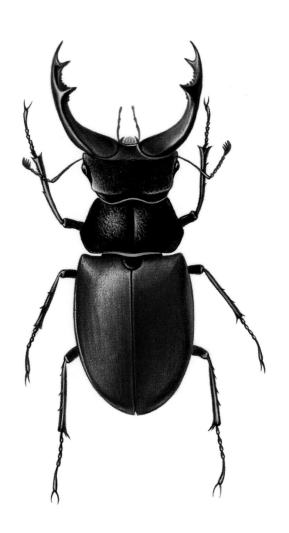

Treecreepers

These common and widespread woodland birds are most readily located by their distinctive call, a high-pitched '*tsee-tsee-tsee*', which is delivered as they shuffle mouse-like along a branch or around the trunk of a tree. Treecreepers have stiff tail feathers, like woodpeckers, to support them as they climb, probing within the bark for insects with their finely curved bill.

Badgers

Eurasian badgers are easily recognisable mammals, and have conspicuous black and white facial markings. They are stocky, omnivorous animals, feeding on everything from rodents and frogs to beetles, berries and seeds. During the autumn, when the animals are trying to build up fat reserves before winter, fruit forms an important energy-rich part of the diet, and the animals will readily forage within orchards for windfall apples, plums, cherries and pears.

By arrangement with the Herts and Middlesex Badger Group, it is possible to watch these animals from a specially erected hide at Tewin Orchard in Hertfordshire. Between April and October, the wardens leave out food each night, and, in addition to badgers, fortunate visitors can expect to see foxes, bats and muntjac deer.

3-4 individuals
around entrance
to sett at
any one
time

very distinctive appearance
from behind
with white
tipped
ears

pausing mid
scratch

peering from sett

© J Chatterton '02

Badgers May 2002
Forest of Dean, Gloucs.

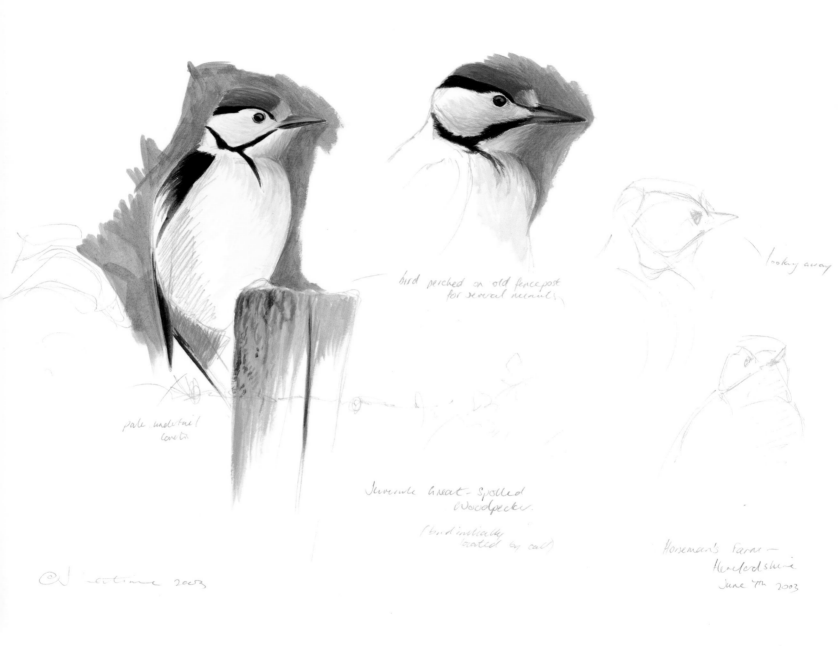

pale undertail
coverts

bird perched on old fencepost
for several minutes

looking away

Juvenile Great-Spotted
Woodpecker.

(bird initially
located by call)

Horseman's Farm –
Herefordshire
June 7th 2003

© J Lortimore 2003

Great Spotted Woodpecker

The great spotted woodpecker is the most numerous and familiar member of the woodpecker family found in Britain. Marginally larger than a starling, these pied birds are common and widespread breeders in traditional orchards, woodland and parkland in England and Wales, though their distribution is more scattered in Scotland and they are completely absent from Ireland.

I remember as a boy longing to see one of these handsome birds. Despite spending hours searching for them in suitable woodland habitat, I frequently left

frustrated, and at times believed the day would never come. Typically, since my first sighting, I now see them frequently and they always delight. Although this species' drumming is a distinctive sound of spring, the birds' call, a short, explosive 'chip', can be heard throughout the year and is a useful clue in determining the presence of a nearby individual. Both birds that are sketched opposite were initially located by such a call and were observed in separate Herefordshire orchards in early spring.

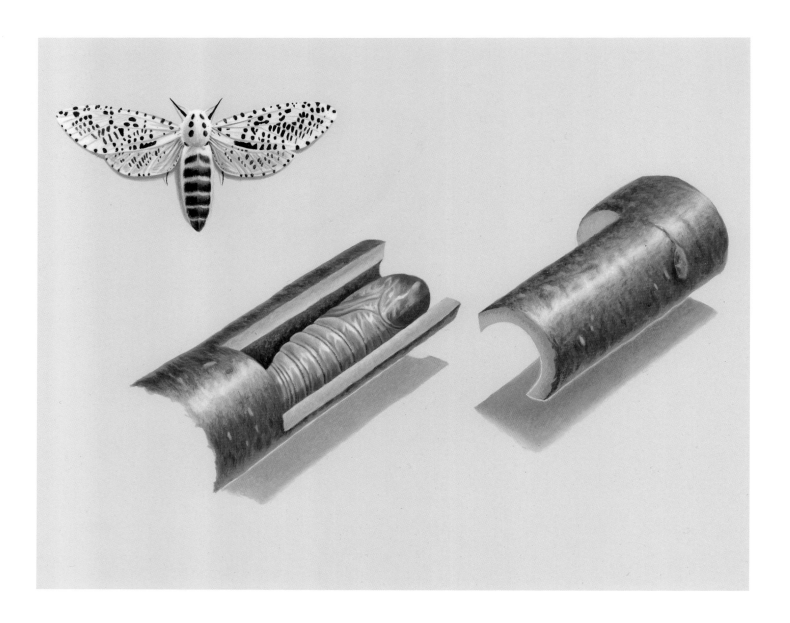

Leopard Moth

Fruit trees suffer from a variety of natural diseases, such as canker and scab. Like other deciduous trees, they are also prone to attack from insects, including the leopard moth, *Zeuzera pyrina*. The caterpillar feeds within the stem tissue of trees, often taking two or three years to reach maturity, before pupating beneath the surface of the bark [illustrated]. Their burrowing causes leaf wilt, and eventually the affected branch may die. If the trunk is attacked, the tree can be killed.

Plum, cherry, hawthorn, apple and pear trees may all be affected by this common resident species, alongside oak, beech and elm. Although the adult moths are nocturnal, both sexes can occasionally be found resting on a tree trunk during the day. The larger female is shown here.

Codling Moth

The codling moth, *Cydia pomonella*, is a notorious fruit pest and is widespread in the British Isles, except in the extreme north of Scotland. It can often be found in orchards and gardens, generally occurring wherever apples are cultivated. The female lays the eggs on the surface of the fruit; the pale pink caterpillar bores into the developing apple and feeds on the central core. The grub can be found inside the fruit in July and August, after which time it overwinters in the bark before pupating the following spring, sometimes within the leaf litter. Moths are usually on the wing in July and August, although a second brood occasionally appears in the autumn. The adults rest on tree trunks and foliage by day and fly at dusk. In addition to apples, the codling moth will also attack the fruits of pear and plums.

Red Admirals and plums.
September 2003.

Early Windfalls

From late July, butterflies and an assortment of other insects are attracted to piles of fermenting plums, in the promise of a sugar-rich meal. The sight of these beautiful and delicate creatures feeding avidly amongst the fallen fruit presents one of the most striking and enduring images I have seen in the preparation of this book.

In a bid to entice feeding butterflies to my garden, a pile of over-ripe plums was placed on a small patch of lawn. Over the following few days, a steady stream of visitors was attracted to the fruit, including many red admirals, comma, painted lady, small tortoiseshell and the occasional speckled wood. As an artist, the opportunity to study wild creatures at such close quarters is immensely useful and enjoyable.

Bird Shapes

I have returned to The Standards orchard, at Moccas in Herefordshire, to do some sketching. A visit earlier in the week produced some good birds, including nuthatches, buzzards and a green woodpecker. Settling down beside the enormous trunk of a perry pear, there is already much to see. Starlings feed noisily on the fallen fruit, and there are chaffinches and great tits amongst them. Every so often the starlings erupt from the floor without warning, filling the sky with an explosion of beating wings, before wheeling above the trees only to alight within the crown of a nearby tree. I can hear the occasional meow of a buzzard overhead, whilst on the orchard floor, squirrels, jays, magpies and several carrion crows pick their way amongst the trees. The orchard seems to be alive with birds, and it is a real joy to be here.

From amongst the foliage above my head comes the incessant 'tic, tic, tic' of a particularly inquisitive robin. Robins are one of my favourite birds. They have so much character, and I am fascinated by just how many poses and postures these birds can adopt. In talking about his drawing, the wildlife artist John Busby describes his enthusiasm for 'collecting bird shapes', and when watching this bird, I understand fully what he means.

Winter Thrushes

Redwings and fieldfares are common and widespread winter visitors to Britain. Small numbers of both species breed in northern Scotland each year, though the birds are most likely to be encountered from late autumn, as large numbers arrive from their breeding grounds in Scandinavia. They feed on insects and worms, with open countryside, including short pasture and ploughed fields, being occupied in winter. Berries, especially hawthorn, are favoured when the birds first arrive, and hedgerows can be stripped in minutes by large flocks, sometimes thousands strong. These gatherings may include other species of thrush, such as blackbirds and, occasionally, in late autumn, ring ouzels.

Fieldfares and redwings are commonly associated with orchards, where they feed avidly on windfall fruit. Grubs and worms are generally preferred, but birds switch to apples and berries when these invertebrates are unavailable. Dessert apples are preferred, but cider varieties, with higher tannin contents, will be taken, especially in hard weather. Occasionally, birds that have over-indulged on fermenting fruit are found intoxicated and allow close approach. Records of individuals found in this condition are relatively common. After a period of 'sobering up', the birds rarely exhibit any negative side effects, other than disorientation, and can be released back into the wild.

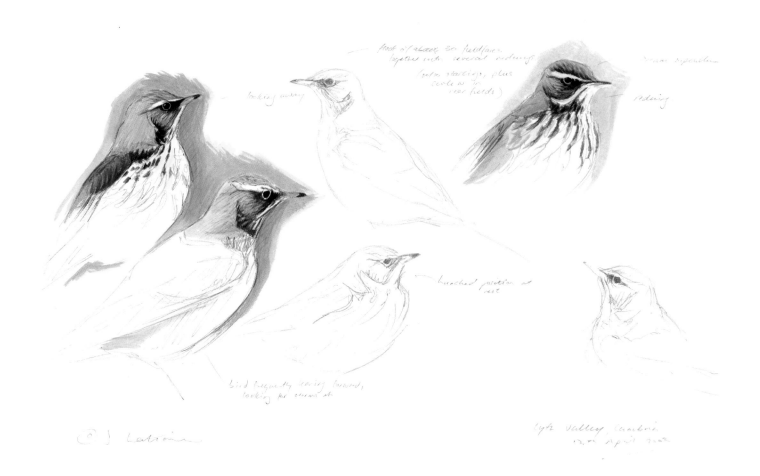

flock of about 30 fieldfares
together with several redwings
(plus starlings, plus
scolts in
near fields)

looking away

redwing

hunched position at
rest

bird frequently leaning forward,
looking for worms etc.

© J Lodoin

Lyth Valley, Cumbria
13th April 2002

thick, cream supercilium
giving bird very
handsome appearance

hunched up bird,
looking as if has
no neck.

red coverts not always
as evident as most
text books suggest

Redwing studies.
The Hyde (old standard orchard)
Nr. Leominster, Herefordshire
16th October 2005

© J Lodoin

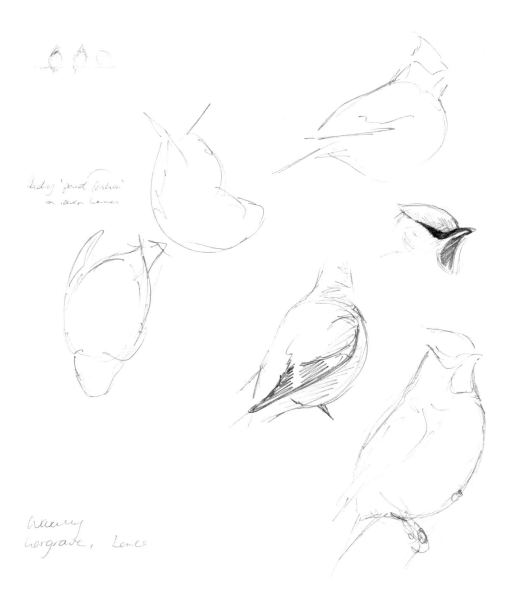

Waxwings

Waxwings are birds of northern Europe, breeding in the remote coniferous forests of Scandinavia, Latvia, Estonia and western Russia. They are generally infrequent winter visitors to Britain, but occasionally appear in huge numbers, usually following a successful breeding season that coincides with a poor autumn berry crop. During such irruptions, the birds quickly strip berry-laden trees like the rowan, often moving into gardens when other food sources are exhausted. At such times, fruit, including crab apples, will readily be taken.

Crab Apples

The crab apple is a generic term generally applied to trees producing small, hard fruits that are often used for making jelly. In their natural state they are bitter and unpalatable to humans, but are readily gorged on by several bird species, not least because the fruits remain on the tree well into winter, constituting a welcome natural bounty.

Unidentified, Malus
type crab apple
(lifesize)

golden yellow ripening
on the tree.

Crab apples, 'John Downie'
August 2003

Jonathan Latimer

Cider and Perry

Cider and Perry

The counties of Herefordshire, Gloucestershire, Worcestershire, Somerset and Devon are famous for their cider apples and, more locally, perry pears, which have been used to make fermented drinks for more than a thousand years. Over the centuries, in excess of 260 cultivars have been developed for use as cider apples, although many varieties have disappeared due to the felling of countless traditional orchards during the First World War, when every bit of good land was ploughed. From a peak during the 1700s and 1800s, cider making has been transformed from a largely cottage industry to a modern, highly sophisticated multi-million-pound global industry. Despite technological advances, both cider and perry continue to be made in traditional ways that have remained relatively unchanged for centuries, although, today, machinery has largely replaced hand labour.

Harvesting of early-ripening fruit begins during September and may last for several weeks, depending upon maturation dates of the varieties grown. Traditionally, prior to milling, the fruit was piled into small mounds, or tumps, and left within the orchard for a period of between two and six weeks to mellow. The softened fruit was then placed in a circular stone trough or 'chase' and crushed by the action of a millstone running in it, the latter rotated with the help of a horse in harness. The pulp was then gathered in large cloths made of horsehair known as 'hairs'. Today, although made of synthetic fibre, they are still referred to as hairs. A dozen of these would be placed on top of one another in a screw press, building a 'cheese'. The juice was then squeezed out of this cheese under pressure (in a traditional twin-screw press, a horizontal timber beam, held within a solid frame, was 'lowered' on to the enclosed pulp mass, in a similar way to how some corkscrews operate), and transferred into wooden casks; the spent pulp residue, known as pomace, was later used for cattle feed. Within a couple of days the juice began to ferment under the influence of naturally occurring yeasts, and after a period of six weeks the casks would be sealed with wooden bungs and left to mature for at least two months. This unsophisticated 'farm cider', or 'scrumpy', is still available today from many of the smaller farmhouse producers, and is usually dispensed directly from the barrel.

Cider Tools

A selection of traditional cider-making tools, from the Museum of Rural Life in Glastonbury, Somerset. The wooden shovel was used to transfer the crushed fruit from the mill to the press, where the edges of the cheese, sometimes made of hay, would be trimmed using a hay knife. The wooden tunnacre, also known as a tun dish, with its funnel-like base, ensured that none of the juice was lost when being poured into the casks prior to fermentation.

Farming and Cider

From the cider-producing monasteries of the past to the farms of pre-war Britain (First World War), cider played an important role in the rural economy of the land for nearly a thousand years. Farms everywhere would have their individual orchards: an area of dry land situated close to the house, which provided sheltered grazing for livestock in addition to all the fruit that it produced. Despite having a selection of eating and cooking apples, the largest proportion of land would be given over to cider apples, which supplied an invaluable yearly crop. A daily allowance of about half a gallon (2–3 litres) constituted a large proportion of a labourer's weekly wage. Available throughout the year, cider was especially welcomed during the busiest times of haymaking and harvesting, and was claimed to be the only drink that enabled a man to work all day in the heat of the harvest field. Whether this is true or not, without the luxury of modern-day machinery, eighteenth- and nineteenth-century farming would certainly have been hard and gruelling work. Unlike beer, which would naturally promote nausea and excessive sweating, cider refreshed and sustained the busy labourers, and during this most demanding time of year, would be served in unlimited quantities. Working long hours, and drinking up to a staggering two gallons a day, it is hardly surprising that accidents were common and occasionally serious. So important was cider as a component of the basic daily wage, alongside farmhouse bread and cheese, that farmers producing little or inferior produce would find it almost impossible to attract seasonal, temporary labour.

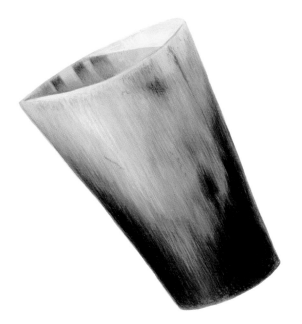

Cider given to farm workers would be served in individual wooden bottles, known as firkins in the West Country and costrels in Herefordshire. Taken into the fields in which the farmers laboured, these containers occasionally included a horn beaker from which to drink.

Blossom Time

An apple orchard at blossom time is truly beautiful. With delicate pink flowers varying in shade from near white to deep pink, parts of the Herefordshire countryside are transformed during the month of May. In the middle of the month, with trees in full bloom, the area around Marcle Ridge attracts visitors from near and far to join in the seasonal celebrations, held in an area famed for its orchards of cider fruit, in addition to dessert and culinary varieties.

During blossom-time celebrations, special events are organised, including cider tasting in nearby Putley Village Hall, where an array of traditional ciders and perries from Herefordshire and surrounding counties are available for sampling. Local cider makers open their orchards, where the public can have a picnic beneath the trees or simply wander along the blossom trails with or without a local guide. With homemade food and entertainment, including traditional Leominster Morris dancers, the whole weekend celebrates the natural beauty, cultural richness and economic importance of orchards in the parishes of the 'Marcle Ridge'.

The bush orchards of Knight's Cider Co. Ltd, based near the village of Storridge and in the shadow of the magnificent Malvern Hills, show the typically strict, regimented rows of closely packed trees, planted between alleyways of neatly cropped turf. Such arrangements are designed to allow access for farm machinery during the year, from spraying during spring to mechanical harvesting in autumn. With many orchards situated within open areas of countryside that support large concentrations of rabbits, buzzards are a common sight throughout rural Worcestershire and Herefordshire, and are birds that I have seen at almost every orchard that I have visited across the country. These raptors are important in helping to control populations of rabbits and other rodents, such as mice and voles, which often resort to gnawing tree bark during the winter months when other preferred food supplies have dwindled.

Although rabbits enjoy eating tender branch tips, in winter they can attack the unprotected trunks of young trees, and remove strips of bark. Severely damaged in this way, trees will show loss of vigour or, in extreme cases, may die.

Cider Apples

Cider apple varieties are categorised on the basis of their juice into four distinctive groups, bittersweets, bittersharps, sweets and sharps. Medaille d'Or is a full bittersweet, having both a high sugar content and a high tannin content. Bittersharps, like the famous Kingston Black, are also high in tannin but have high acidity levels. As their name suggests, sweets are high in sugar and have occasionally been used in the past as eating apples, for example Sweet Coppin. They are low in tannin. Tom Putt is a good example of a sharp cider apple and, being low in tannin and high in acid, is generally similar to culinary apples in taste. As such, this variety is often categorised as a dual-purpose apple. Cider is mainly produced using a blend of various varieties of apple, to give a more balanced flavour, but some apples, like the Kingston Black, will produce a distinctive full-bodied drink on its own.

Most of these varieties were collected in Herefordshire with the help of Chris Fairs, from commercial orchards that he has helped to plant and manage over the last 30 years. Having never seen cider apples before my autumn visit to the county, I was both surprised and fascinated by the variation in their size, shape and colour.

Left column, from top: Brown's apple, Bulmer's Norman, Dabinett, Ellis Bitter

Middle from top: Reinette O'bry, Tom Putt, Yarlington Mill, Sweet Coppin

Right from top: Broxwood Foxwhelp, Michelin, Cider Lady's Finger, Kingston Black, Brown Snout

Left: apple illustrated at life size, though fruits will vary greatly according to the age of the tree and the cropping year. Younger trees tend to produce much larger specimens than mature trees, whilst many varieties of apple are notoriously biennial bearers, which, without control, produce a few large, early-ripening fruit in the off year and a large crop of much smaller, later-maturing fruit the following season.

Woodpecker Cider

Percy Bulmer introduced Woodpecker Cider to the world in 1894, just seven years after he founded his company in Herefordshire, England, at the age of twenty. Named after the bird that he regularly saw in the apple orchard at his father's rectory, it was his first successful branded cider and remains, to this day, the sweetest of the drinks in the Bulmer range. With a £1000 loan from their father, Percy and his elder brother, Fred, bought an eight-acre field just outside the city walls and built their first cider mill. Compared with the huge, computer-controlled, present-day steel plant, this would have been little more than a primitive wooden shack. Using only the wild yeasts naturally present within the skin of the apple, cider making in the early days was very much a hit-or-miss affair. It was not long, though, before Dr Herbert Durham isolated a selected strain, and the first pure cider yeast culture was created, thus ensuring that all future fermentations were consistent. It was the start of commercial cider making. Today Bulmers, the biggest cider makers in the world, make 65% of the five million hectolitres sold annually in the UK.

This painting has been reprodcued with the kind premission of Bulmers, Hereford

Tree shaking on an industrial scale

Tractors

Tractors play an important role in the modern, mechanised process of cider apple production. Employed for spraying and mowing during the growing season, they are fully utilised in the autumn when undertaking tree shaking, harvesting, and hauling fruit to the loading pad. Here the fruit is stored before being sent to the factory, ideally within a period of 48 hours. In a typical bush orchard, 50–100 tonnes of fruit a day can be harvested using a large tractor-mounted harvester, assisted by a second 'hauling' tractor and two trailers.

Many of the compact, narrow tractors used in modern bush orchards are bought specifically for the purpose, as they are able to work within the confines of intensively planted tree rows. Often incorporating four-wheel drive for good traction, they require sufficient horsepower (commonly 80–90 bhp) to carry and drive a cider apple harvester and simultaneously

tow a three-ton trailer load of fruit.

Tractors, and the modern machines and implements fitted to them, have had an enormous impact on the output and efficiency of cider apple production. This is particularly true of the apple harvest, a time of peak labour demand. There is insufficient economically priced labour available today for a farmer to contemplate the hand harvesting of fruit in a large bush tree orchard. This becomes clear when one compares the handpicking rate, typically 1–1.5 tonnes/day, with the ability of the machine, quoted in an earlier paragraph. For tree shaking itself, the contrast is even more startling. One could expect a strong man to be able to shake between 5 and 10 trees an hour, but by the end of the morning, his work rate would certainly lessen. In comparison, a mechanical tree shaker with an experienced operator can, without ever slowing, shake 200 trees an hour!

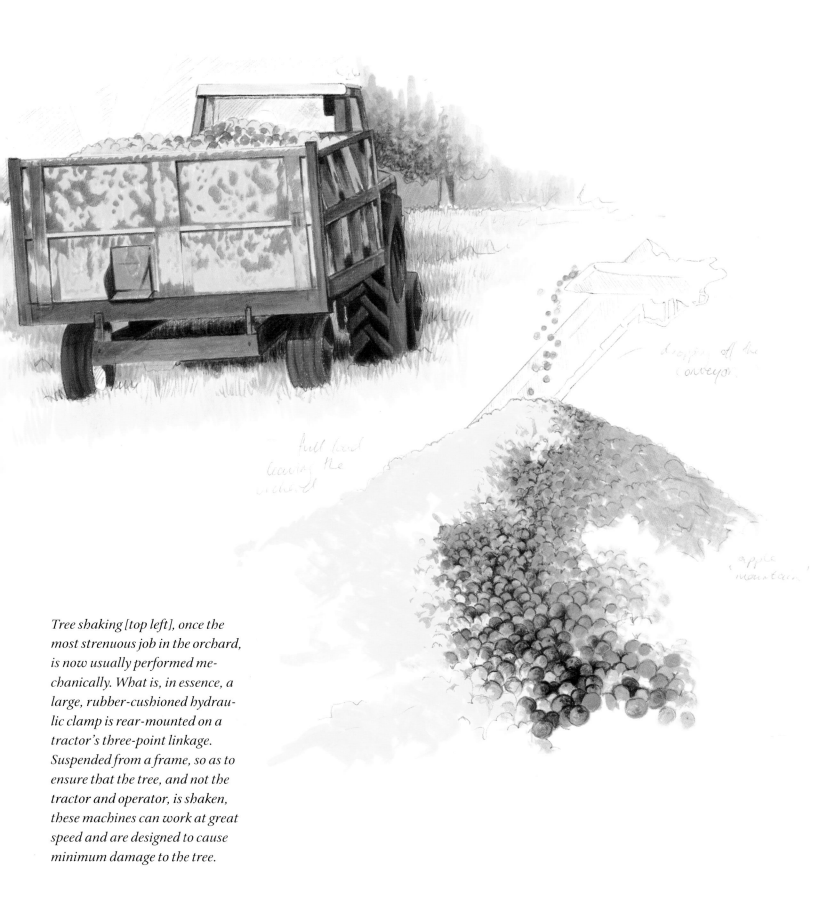

Tree shaking [top left], once the most strenuous job in the orchard, is now usually performed mechanically. What is, in essence, a large, rubber-cushioned hydraulic clamp is rear-mounted on a tractor's three-point linkage. Suspended from a frame, so as to ensure that the tree, and not the tractor and operator, is shaken, these machines can work at great speed and are designed to cause minimum damage to the tree.

Westons Cider

Situated in the Herefordshire village of Much Marcle, Westons Cider is based at 'The Bounds', the original 17th-century farm bought by the company's founder, Henry Weston, in 1878. The firm is still run by the Weston family, and produces 40 different types of cider and perry, selling a total of approximately 1.4 million gallons a year. These brands are not only available throughout the UK, but are also exported to 14 countries worldwide.

Most of the fruit is supplied from farms within a 15-mile radius of the company – the 70 acres of Weston's orchards providing about 10% of their yearly requirements. Having been delivered, the fruit is milled and then pressed on a state-of-the-art Bucher-Guyer Press, installed at the turn of the century, and capable of extracting 175 gallons (795 litres) of juice from each ton of pulp pressed. The liquid is then pumped into holding tanks, to await testing for sugar and acidity content, before being stored in oak vats where the process of fermentation begins. The 80 vats have a total capacity of 5.5 million litres. Champagne yeast strains, similar to those used in wine making, are used to turn the juice. When fermented, the cider is left to mature in the vats, before blending takes place.

The visitor's centre and shop is open all year round, and includes The Henry Weston Garden – an award-winning feature, originally exhibited at the Hampton Court Palace Flower show in 2002. Organised tours of the mill are run throughout the year, and a selection of Weston's ciders and perries can be enjoyed at the Scrumpy House Restaurant & Bar.

Shire horse dray rides take place throughout the summer months and are pulled by resident shire horses, 'Senator' and 'Nobby'.

Broome Farm

Broome Farm, home to John and Hilary Draper, is a
working cider farm with 45 acres of cider apple orchard at Peterstow, near the historic market town of
Ross-on-Wye, in Herefordshire. The county has over
10,000 acres of cider orchards, which produce 286
million litres of cider per year – half the total output
of the UK. Offering bed and breakfast, Broome Farm
makes an excellent base from which to document the
cider apple harvest. Here I have arranged to meet
Chris Fairs, who works for H.P. Bulmer as a Growers'
Advisory Manager, offering cider fruit suppliers
a free technical service, covering everything
from pre-planting advice to general orchard
management and fruit delivery.

I first met Chris at an orchard conference at
Tatton Park in Cheshire, where he offered to
help with my research. Having worked in
the Orcharding Department of Bulmer's
since 1971, Chris has an intimate knowledge of the local area, and has known the
Drapers for many years, since the majority of the fruit harvested from their
orchards is contracted to the company.
Over coffee and toast in the Broome
farmhouse kitchen, we study his well-
planned itinerary before it is time to
begin some work.

*Mike Johnson, Hilary's brother, manages
the orchards at Broome Farm.*

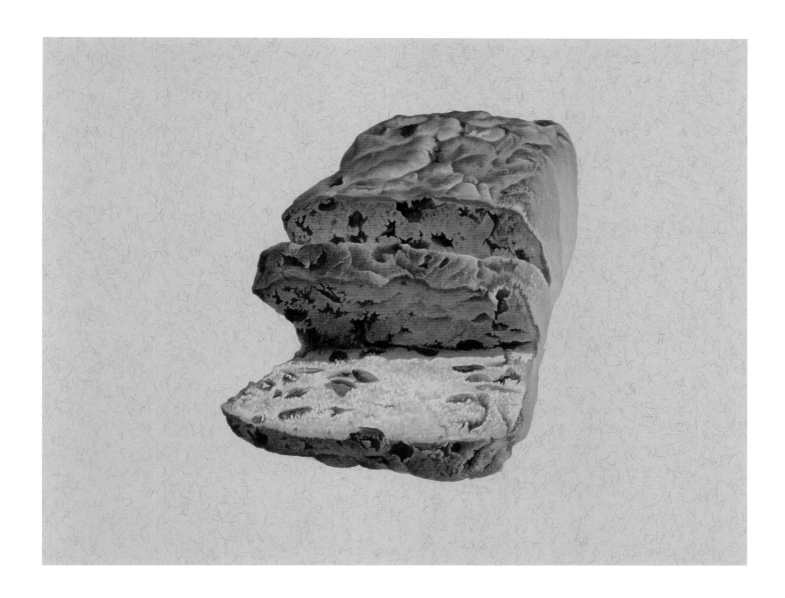

Cider Cake

The licensed dining room at Broome Farm provides delicious food for bed and breakfast guests and is also open to the public. People travel for miles around to enjoy the cream teas and homemade cider cake, which is made using Mike's home-produced cider and apples grown on the farm.

INGREDIENTS:

8oz sultanas
¼ pt 'Broome Farm Cider'
4oz margarine
4oz soft brown sugar (light)
2 eggs
8oz self-raising flour
2tsp mixed spice
1 large Bramley apple (chopped)

METHOD:

Soak the sultanas in cider overnight. Mix all the remaining ingredients together, adding the sultanas at the end. Cook in a 2lb loaf tin for approximately 1.5 hrs at 150°C

Autumn at 'The Broome'

The Orchards at Broome Farm have grown considerably in size under the stewardship of Mike Johnson, with over 10,000 additional trees planted since the mid 1990s. The majority of the fruit harvested comprises Michelin and Dabinett apples, which are favoured by large-scale commercial growers. However, more traditional varieties such as Broxwood Foxwhelp and Kingston Black are also found on the farm. Mike has successfully been producing cider and perry for a number of years, and six acres have been set aside with traditional cider apple and perry pear varieties, to be used specifically for this purpose. The resultant produce, both bottled and straight from the barrel, are available at the farm.

My last night at The Broome and I am able to watch Mike at work. It is barely seven o'clock and, after some supper, I venture outside into the darkness of the yard. The light from the barn indicates that Mike is around, and I find him preparing the apples whilst finishing the last of his lunch.

The farm is such a busy place at this time of year, with harvesting and haulage of contract fruit to be organised, that there is little time to eat. Any of his own cider or perry making tends to be neglected until the rest of the work is done. Many bags of fruit are now stacked up against the trees, and Mike is anxious to get started before the critical 'milling period' for each variety is passed, after which the fruit becomes too spoiled to use.

Milling

The fruit is initially washed to remove dirt and any organic debris by dipping a large plastic tray – a glorified sieve – into a water-filled vat. The tray is then lifted out and stacked until the fruit is ready to be poured into the funnel-like mouth of the mill, which is driven by a tractor. After milling for less than a minute, the well-churned, resultant pulp slops heavily into a large plastic barrel below. It looks foul, a cross between thick, lumpy apple sauce and peanut butter. When the barrel is full, the final stage, pressing, is almost ready to begin.

Building the cheese

A wooden frame, about two feet square and eight inches high, is lined with hessian sacking and placed on a stainless steel basin, which is connected by hydraulic hose to the tractor. Pulp is poured into the frame, then spread out and levelled off by hand. The overhanging corners of sacking are folded over, holding the pulp in an envelope-like sleeve. The wooden frame holding this mass can then be removed and the pile covered with a thin ash board, known as a slat. (Ash is used as it becomes flexible when wet and will not break under pressure.) The process is repeated until a 'cheese' is completed and ready for pressing. Soon the juice begins to flow from the shrinking mass into a waiting bucket below. The collected liquid is then poured into a selected barrel, in which fermentation will take place. Once the cider has stopped 'working', the barrel will be completely sealed to await the final process – blending.

Watching milling and pressing for the first time is a fascinating experience. Although the hardware may differ from farm to farm, the basic principles of extracting juice from the fruit remain the same for traditional producers of cider and perry across the country.

Blending

Once pressed, many cider producers hold the raw juice in tanks to await testing for sugar content and the levels of acidity and sulphides present. In the laboratory at Weston's Cider, staff are charged with the task of turning the juice into award-winning cider. Analysis continues through fermentation, noting the acid and alcohol content of the new cider. These key factors disclose the character of the liquid and indicate the type of cider that the juice will become. The methods adopted are the same as those used by Customs and Excise and provide the most accurate measurements of a cider's contents.

Although many smaller cider and perry producers do not have the infrastructure for such rigorous testing, the developing cider is sampled regularly, usually in the morning when the taster's palate is at its freshest. Frequent evaluation of the cider's subtle character changes helps to determine when fermentation is complete. (It is possible to detect this latter stage by ear, as the hissing and bubbling noises emitted during fermentation will cease.) Experienced tasters judge the cider on flavour, aroma and alcohol content, which together indicate the individual characteristics of the cider or blend contained within each vat. When fermentation is over, the juice is compared with a 'standard' blended sample. To match it, different ciders are mixed to achieve the desired result – a drier, sweeter or more alcoholic drink. When judged to be ready, the cider is passed through a series of filters to remove any remaining fine organic matter*, to leave a clear and fresh product that is ready to drink.

* Some producers forego these latter processes of blending and filtration, to create a traditional farmhouse 'scrumpy'.

Perry Pears

Like cider apples, perry pears can be classified into four main categories, sweet, medium-sharp, bittersweet and bittersharp (astringent-sharp). Sweet and medium-sharp pears, like Bartestree Squash and Gin, have low acidity and tannin contents. There are only a few varieties of bittersweet pears. These have much higher tannin contents than other categories of pears. Bittersharps, like Oldfield, have a high acidity content, with a very harsh, astringent taste, which helps to produce the best-quality perry. Perry pears have some wonderfully descriptive names, such as Stinking Bishop or Flakey Bark, whilst the Holmer pear is colloquially known as 'Startlecock' because of its high diuretic properties.

Most of these pears were collected at Broome Farm and were identified with the help of Mike Johnson.

Top row, left to right:
Blakeney Red, Gin, Bartestree Squash

Second row: Turner's Barn, Sickle Pear, Oldfield

Third row: Barland, Aylton Red, Butt

Bottom: Barnett, Holmer, Hendre Huffcap, White Bache

Above: illustrated life-size

Traditional Harvesting

During the autumn, casual staff are hired to help with the harvest. Fallen fruit is gathered from the ground into sacks, ready for milling, whilst long poles are used to shake the branches to remove remaining fruit from the trees. In contrast to apples and pears for cooking and eating, which become unusable (at least on a commercial level) when bruised, fruit used in cider and perry making is frequently damaged during harvesting. This matters little, as everything from the pip to the skin is ultimately crushed and pressed. Badly damaged fruit that has been left to rot for any length of time on the ground will begin to ferment under the influence of naturally occurring yeasts. If possible, this fruit is removed by hand and discarded from the process.

Mike's border collie, Fizz, is constantly at his side as he goes around the farm.

The Standards Orchard at Moccas in Herefordshire boasts a number of huge perry pear trees. These trees generally have a greater longevity than apple trees, which normally die after 80–120 years. Some standard perry pear trees might begin to bear fruit after three years, although they may not start to yield a respectable harvest for 30 years or be 'mature' until 70 years of age or more. This point of maturity is difficult to define and will depend on several factors, such as the rootstock, tree variety, depth of soil and planting density. Many specimens will continue to produce a crop until the last root connection is severed or they die of disease, at perhaps 200, or occasionally 300, years of age. The larger cider apple trees within this orchard were planted prior to 1930 by Mr Bill Whiting for the Moccas Estate, and include Bulmer's Norman and Yarlington Mill. The older perry pears were planted more than 100 years before this, and they are stunning to behold. At least 170 years old, it is remarkable to think that some of these trees were producing a crop before Queen Victoria had come to the throne.

Under the direction of Colin Hinksman, who took over the tenancy of the orchard in 1998, the orchard has undergone a rapid renovation, with more than 260 new trees planted under the Stewardship Scheme. Through grant aids to specific landscape types, the scheme is aimed at improving the natural beauty and diversity of the countryside for the benefit of wildlife and people alike. This mixed-variety orchard, recently planted with varieties such as Bramley, Katy and Chisel Jersey, seems to be alive with birds. There are robins and starlings, mixed flocks of tits, thrushes and large numbers of crows.

Colin is knowledgeable about the wildlife in the area and is keen to see what I have recorded on paper. After chatting for a while about the orchard, he begins the work of harvesting the fallen fruit, which is done using a large, hand-operated picker. If left for too long on the orchard floor, the pears may well spoil, and be unusable for perry making. In a few minutes, I hear the heavy 'chug, chug, chug' of the picker as it starts up. Not unlike a large, old-fashioned and bulbous-looking lawnmower in appearance, the harvester looks quite cumbersome to use, though its effectiveness in collecting fruit from the orchard floor is demonstrated by the speed with which the large basket fitted on the side of the machine is filled. Having been collected and later bagged, the fruit will be sent to a local perry producer.

Cider-making Festival

At the Cider Museum in Hereford, an annual Cider-making Festival takes place in October, in conjunction with apple day events across the country. Lying within the heart of Britain's cider-making counties, Herefordshire has a special association with the drink, and became the principle region for cider production in the 1600s. It was then that Lord Scudamore introduced the Redstreak apple, after taking an interest in orchard husbandry during his stay in France as Ambassador to Charles I.

With mild springs, warm summers and gentle rainfall in autumn, Herefordshire's climate is excellent for large-scale apple growing. It is no surprise, then, that Hereford is home to H.P. Bulmer, the largest cider manufacturer in the world, which mills and presses in excess of 1500 tons of fruit daily during the autumn.

The Cider Museum is housed in part of the company's former Ryelands Street Factory, and chronicles the fascinating history of traditional cider making in the area. Here there are displays featuring everything from early presses and huge oak vats, to the famous Herefordshire Pomona, a beautifully illustrated book featuring many of the cider apple varieties grown in the county. The book was compiled and published during the late nineteenth century, resulting from work carried out by Dr Robert Hogg, who was commissioned to survey the entire county's orchards when cider making was in some decline.

The festival hosts an assortment of different stalls, offering family activities including apple pressing for children, and a display of traditional dancing, complete with authentic seventeenth-century attire. Centre stage goes to a traditional cider-making demonstration from Ralph's Cider, based in New Radnor, Powys. I am able to observe the entire process from different viewpoints in the open air. This is both useful and informative, and, after producing some quick sketches that can be worked up later, I watch as the freshly pressed juice is finally poured into large oak vats for fermentation to begin.

Ralph's Cider

Ralph Owen, demonstrating traditional cider making at the Hereford Cider Museum. A tractor-driven mill is used to crush the apples; the resultant pulp is pressed in a wheel-mounted, twin-screw press. In the 1800s, travelling cider makers would be a familiar sight during the autumn, towing hand-operated mills and presses from farm to farm, processing the fruit of growers with no equipment of their own. Some cider makers were still operating as late as 1950. Today, traditional cider making can be witnessed at country shows and beer festivals nationwide.

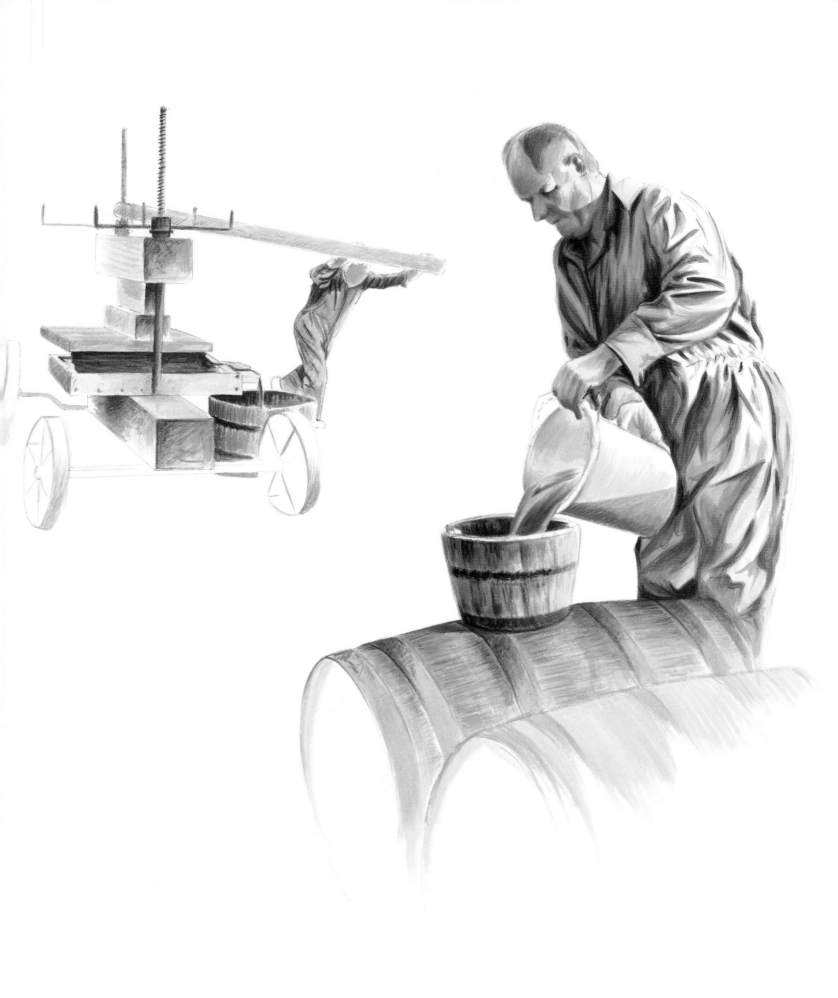

Somerset Cider

The association between Somerset and cider is strong and deep-rooted, the first recorded cider presses dating back to the early thirteenth century. It was 400 years later that the Long Parliament imposed the first levy on the county's 'golden claret'. In 1763, under the leadership of Prime Minister Lord Bute, cider levies rose to help finance the Seven Years' War. Without the need of a warrant, tax collectors were given the right to enter homes to seize unpaid taxes. The West Country citizens rose up in rebellion, marching in the streets and burning effigies of the Prime Minister. 'An Englishman's home is his castle!' proclaimed William Pitt the Elder, and, finally, in an embarrassing political climbdown, Lord Bute was forced to resign from power, though not before sending in the army to quell the demonstrations.

The levy on cider was eventually reduced, and, over the next hundred years, the drink's popularity grew. Towards the end of the nineteenth century, the planting of orchards for cider production was at its height, with Somerset boasting 24,000 acres of orchard set aside for this purpose. Despite the fact that Somerset retains its strong links with the drink, less than 10% of the county's orchards now remain, an inevitable result of changing farm practices, as other crops have became more profitable, and the increasing pressure on land for housing and development. EU grants have further encouraged orchards to be grubbed, owing to overproduction.

On a more positive note, interest in conserving traditional orchards and the culture surrounding Somerset's cider production is being revived. Displays documenting its history also help to inform the public. David Walker, the curator at The Rural Life Museum in Glastonbury, is enthusiastic about the cider-making past and is keen to share his knowledge. The centrepiece of the museum is the fourteenth-century Tithe Barn. This and other buildings surrounding the central courtyard illustrate the different farming techniques of Victorian Somerset, including peat digging and mud horse fishing. The traditional farmhouse orchard adjacent to the museum supplies a variety of different cider apples, which are utilised in milling demonstrations in the autumn.

Cider Shoe

In cider-producing counties like Somerset, heated cider was often served in local pubs and taverns. The 'cider shoe', generally made from copper or perhaps brass or tin, would be thrust into the hot coals of an open fire to heat the drink. Additional ingredients such as ginger or gin were frequently added to produce a spicy, heart-warming tipple.

Wilkins' Farmhouse Cider

It is mid-November and there is hardly a cloud in the sky on this glorious late autumn day. After spending the morning at the Somerset Rural Life Museum, I have come to Mudgley, about five miles to the west of Glastonbury, to visit Roger Wilkins, of Wilkins' Farmhouse Cider. Roger took over the cider business that his grandfather started in back in 1917, and has run the company for the last 35 years.

After leaving my car in the courtyard, I make my way to the open door of the barn, where I find Roger busy at work. Wilkins' produces Dry, Medium and Sweet Farmhouse Cider, and, having already offered me a sample, Roger duly pours me a further half pint: a measure of the generosity for which he is well known. 'If you're not rushing off, we'll be doing some pressing in the next 10 minutes', he says, and, although I have watched traditional milling and pressing on several occasions before, I gladly wait to watch the work begin. Whilst the process remains similar each time, Roger's equipment differs in several respects: most notably in the utilisation of an overhead holding tank, which discharges pulp on to the 'hair' cloths as the 'cheese' is built up. I watch as, in total, 11 layers are stacked, each holding about a hundredweight of milled fruit. Under pressure, the liquid pours from the towering mass in a steady stream, into a huge stainless steel vat within the floor. This is real Somerset cider; there are no yeasts added to those naturally present within the fruit. Collecting a glass of silky orange liquid from the press, it is like no apple juice I have tasted before. It is strong, smooth, and 100% pure.

In addition to housing the cider mill and press, the barn has a selection of barrelled ciders, which can be tasted before purchasing for consumption off the premises. There are vegetables on sale too, a host of locally grown produce, in addition to real Cheddar cheese. Roger used to sell his own freshly pressed apple juice, which had to be drunk within four days, before the process of fermentation began. This has now ceased, as impending recommendations from the Food Standards Agency are likely to maintain that there is a potential risk of contamination in orchards where livestock are grazed. This applies particularly to fresh fruit and unfermented juices. Thankfully, proposals advocating the complete exclusion of grazing animals from traditional orchards have recently been rejected by the FSA. Such guidance would not apply to orchards where fruit is processed exclusively for cider or perry, or where fruit juice is pasteurised, since these procedures are considered to eliminate any risk to health.

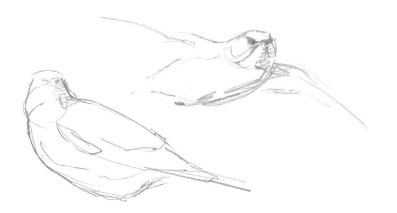

The view across the Levels from the yard is stunning, with the distinctive form of Glastonbury Tor and the town below visible in the hazy distance. Roger joins me outside in the warm November sunshine, where we chat for a while about the orchards and his business. This year seems to have produced a bumper harvest for many people I have talked to, and Roger is no exception. For at least some producers, the scale of the yield has prevented the entire crop from being picked in time for processing, but one thing is certain; with flocks of hungry winter thrushes marauding the Somerset countryside, they certainly won't go to waste.

Behind the courtyard and road the land rises above the farm to join the rolling farmland beyond. This terraced orchard slope is steeper than it first appears, the tangled grass and fallen fruit making the ground very slippery in places, and, on a couple of occasions, I almost loose my footing completely amongst the marble-like carpet of fruit. This probably has more to do with the fact that I am more intent on watching the birds than where I am placing my feet. The distinctive rattle of fieldfares fills the air, whilst every now and then I obtain excellent views of perching birds before they depart silently on outstretched wings above my head. The whole orchard seems to be alive with robins, whilst parties of tits rove noisily amongst the trees. A treecreeper squeaks its way up a sun-bathed trunk like a clockwork mouse, and there are pied wagtails, wood pigeons and mistle thrushes too. Best of all is a green woodpecker, which I flush from the orchard floor before it clatters off through the trees. I think I get more of a surprise than the bird, which remained invisible as it fed intently on the ground. There is a second individual nearby, calling from the trees beyond the ridge. For me, this small, bird-filled orchard, set deep within the Somerset countryside, vividly illustrates the fantastic potential of orchards for attracting wildlife. For an avid birder like me, this is what orchards are all about.

Wassail

Perhaps the most well-known tradition associated with orchards and cider is the Wassail, an annual celebration of music, dance and song. Traditionally celebrated on Twelfth Night, the festivities centred around toasting the good health of the apple trees that would bear the crop for the following year's cider, a mid-winter counterpart to the traditional autumn harvest festival. The word 'wassail' is derived from the Anglo Saxon greeting 'wes hal!', literally meaning 'be in good health!'. Each parish, county and region had its own variations of the celebrations, though firing guns into the air to protect the trees from evil spirits would be commonplace. It is thought that this activity probably helped dislodge insect pests, thus ensuring a bumper crop in the coming season. The oldest tree would form the centrepiece of proceedings, representing the entire orchard. Pieces of bread were soaked in cider and placed in the tree's forks. Even more cider was poured on to its roots to encourage growth and prosperity.

Banging drums and blowing whistles were intended to wake the sleeping trees. A communal mug or wassail bowl, from which all would drink, was adorned with ribbons, filled with cider and passed around the participants. The entire occasion was one of celebration and togetherness. Sadly, ceremonies like these have almost died out. However, in some areas they are being revived in a bid to renew community links and country traditions.

A modern, hand-made wassail
mug by John Leach.

Firing guns into the tree canopy is a traditional activity of wassail celebrations. Below, a modern version of a wassail bowl, produced by local craftsman John Leach. Used with permission.

Wassail Song

Great apple tree of red soil deep,

Our wassail hear in winter's sleep.

That on spring's dawn your buds may swell

With blossom proud to set fruit well.

Your laden frame shall shelter give

All livestock that beneath you live;

To tup and bull, fat lamb and cow,

To goose, grey hen and spotted sow.

Prime juice, which from your fruit we mill,

Fine cider makes that none dares spill.

You grow in pasture rich and old,

With deepest roots, upright to hold.

This mighty trunk and branches thick,

We beat tonight with wassail stick,

To evil spirits drive away

Throughout the year to harvest day.

Browned bread, which we in cider steep,

Shall cause within, your sap to leap.

Placed up among these branches strong,

Retain our toast all summer long.

And now from bowl of vintage take,

Assuring you from slumber wake.

A wassail loud we raise, that thee

Should fruitful be, great apple tree.

Wassail!

CHRIS FAIRS, 2002

Glossary

Acre an imperial measure for land, equal to 4047 square meters, or 0.047 hectares

ADAS Agricultural Development and Advisory Service

Biodiversity the sum total of all living organisms, along with their individual variations, and their interactions, which make up the fabric of the planet earth and allow it to function as it does

Colt dwarfing rootstock – dwarfing rootstock used for the propagation of cherries

Common Ground a small national charity formed in 1983, recognised for playing a unique role in the arts and environmental fields in an effort to improve the quality of our everyday places.

Corvids any members of the crow family

Countryside Restoration Trust Cambridge-based charity dedicated to the protection and restoration of the countryside

Gregg's Pit orchard in Much Marcle, so named because of the marl pit there, from which, it is said, the lime mortar was made to point the stonework of the thirteenth-century church of St Bartholomew in the village

Grubbed (grubbing) the act of removing unwanted or unprofitable plantations, especially orchards

Hectare metric unit of area equal to 10,000 square meters, equivalent to 2.471 acres

Hectolitres a metric unit of volume or capacity, equal to 100 litres

Home Counties a semi-archaic name for the English counties bordering London, frequently applied without geographical precision to the south-east of England

Irruption a sudden invasion of birds, animals or insects, usually in large numbers

Loading pad area within an orchard where harvested fruit is stored prior to being taken to factory for processing.

Longevity long life

Medlar small deciduous tree cultivated for its fruit, which resembles crab apples

Mycelium the root-like network of filaments (hyphae) making up the non-reproductive part of the fungus body

Northern Fruit Group based at RHS Harlow Carr Botanical Gardens, Harrogate, dedicated to encouraging fruit growing in the north of England.

Precambrian a geological term denoting the time in Earth's history prior to 570 million years ago.

Red List Species list compiled by the BTO, highlighting species that have undergone a rapid (more than 50%) decline in UK breeding population over last 25 years

Rootstock a root and its associated growth buds, used as the stock in plant grafting to increase vigour and strength of growth

Scandinavia referring to Iceland, Denmark, Finland, Sweden, Norway, and the Faeroe Islands

Silage fodder (livestock feed) prepared by storing and fermenting green forage plants in a silo

Soft fruit general term referring to soft-skinned, juicy fruit growing head-high or smaller, including strawberries, gooseberries, currants, etc

Sustainable development development that meets the needs of the present without compromising the ability of future generations to meet their own needs

Sward the grassy surface of a lawn, pasture or playing field, composed of short grasses

Tannin a natural component found to varying degrees in the skins, seeds and stems of fruits, most prominent in red wines, where it creates a dry, puckering sensation in the mouth

Tithe Barn a barn originally built to hold 'tithes', peasant taxes paid in-kind to the church

Index

References in bold text refer to illustrations.